# Christian Counseling Casebook

GARY R. COLLINS

# Christian Counseling
# Casebook

THOMAS NELSON PUBLISHERS
*Since 1798*

www.thomasnelson.com

*Book design and composition by Mark McGarry, Texas Type & Book Works*
*Set in Meridien*

Library of Congress Cataloging-in-Publication Data
Collins, Gary R.
Christian counseling casebook : a companion to Christian counseling /
Gary R. Collins.
p. cm.
Includes bibliographical references and index.
ISBN 978-1-4185-1660-4 (alk. paper)
1. Pastoral counseling. I. Title.
BV4012.2.C5623 2007
253.5—dc22
2007008902

*Printed in the United States of America*
1 2 3 4 5 — 10 09 08 07

*To the twenty-eight Christian
counselors, pastors, and counselees
who
provided the case stories for this book
and who
agreed to remain anonymous
to help protect the identities of the people
whose life stories are described.*

*You know who you are.*

*The author and the readers of this book
are very grateful for your
unselfish and gracious contributions
to a book that
can help us all be better counselors.*

# Contents

# Introduction

Counseling is an art; it is a skill, based on a body of knowledge and best learned by practice. Good counseling depends on the personalities of the counselors, the competence that comes from their training, the breadth of their experience, the depth of their knowledge, and the degrees to which their counselees cooperate. Good counseling takes time to learn. In practice, counseling can be hard work, in part because it so often is done with people who resist change. At times counseling can be fulfilling; often it can be incredibly frustrating.

Christian counseling may even be harder than more secular approaches because the Christian who counsels needs to have a knowledge of basic theology and biblical principles that can be applied to contemporary problems. According to psychologist Mark McMinn, a knowledge of "orthodox Christian theology keeps counselors grounded in the midst of a profession easily swayed by new theories, fads, and sensationalist claims."* He adds that the best-prepared Christian counselors are highly trained in counseling theory, ethics, and techniques, but they also are knowledgeable about theology. In addition, the maximally effective Christian counselors are men and women whose lives show Christian character, Christian values, and a growing spirituality.

This book is written as a companion to the third edition of *Christian Counseling: A Comprehensive Guide*. Whereas the *Christian Counseling*

* Mark R. McMinn, *Psychology, Theology, and Spirituality in Christian Counseling* (Wheaton, IL: Tyndale House, 1996), 9.

book is a compilation of knowledge concerning basic counseling issues and skills, this casebook is a guidebook to help readers apply their knowledge to real cases. Each of the following chapters presents one (and sometimes more than one) story that illustrates the material that is discussed in *Christian Counseling.* In the appendix at the end of this book, I describe the origin of the cases and the efforts that have been made to protect the identities of the people whose life stories are told.

The cases that follow are intended to represent a diversity of counseling issues. The stories involve people from different ethnic, religious, socio-economic, educational, and age groups. Most of the counselors and their counselees are from North America, but selected cases are from Latin America, the Middle East, Africa, and other parts of the world. Efforts have been made to find case stories that could apply in a variety of cultures. To help accomplish this goal, selected chapters from the manuscript were sent to counselors in different parts of the world to get their reactions in order to develop a book that can be used cross-culturally. Some cases are included because they will call for readers to think how they would counsel in settings very different from what they might encounter in their own communities. These cases are intended to show that counseling methods need to be adapted; rarely, if ever, does one approach apply to every person or to every culture.

Each of the chapters begins with a brief introduction followed by the case story or stories. After these there are three sets of questions. The *Discussion Questions* focus primarily on the case and raise questions about how the counselee might best be helped. The *General Questions* focus more broadly on relevant issues that are suggested by the presented case but may extend beyond the case. The *Personal Reflection Questions* are written for the reader/counselor to reflect on ways in which the case and the topics under discussion could apply personally to the reader.

There are several ways in which this book can be used. First, individual readers can go through each chapter and answer the questions. This can be a valuable learning experience, but for most people learning will be enhanced if several people are involved in working through this book together. This second way to use this book involves small groups of students or counselors reading the cases and answering the discussion questions and the general questions in the group. *Please note that the personal reflection questions are not designed for group discussion. These are personal questions that readers are encouraged to answer privately and on paper, sometimes prior to discussing the answers with a counselor or friend who will be able to keep the conversations confidential.* A third way to use this book is for an entire class or seminar group to interact with the discussion and general questions in the larger setting and under the guidance of a more experienced professor or counselor. Once again, the personal reflection questions are not intended for open discussion. Fourth, the discussion or general questions can be used as examination questions. In this way these become study guides for students who know that they will be presented with one or more of these questions on the examination for the course. Finally, some training programs may want to focus on the personal reflection questions and ask students to write answers that will be read by professors as confidential assignments or as the foundation for individual or group counseling.

In an initial test of these approaches, some of the following chapters were field tested with students, professors, and counselors both in English-speaking parts of North America and in a Latin American country where the cases were translated and discussed in Spanish. I am especially grateful to Kathy Chase and Sergio Mijangos, who took the lead in facilitating this field testing.

In the introduction of a book like this it is customary for authors to thank the people who have contributed to the book's production. This book includes the combined contribution of twenty-eight remarkable and selfless people—mostly counselors—who have provided the cases for this book, critiqued the chapters, and encouraged me in this project in many ways. I would like to list their names and to thank them publicly, but all have agreed that they should remain anonymous to help protect the identities of the people whose stories make up the core of this book. I have dedicated the book to these twenty-eight people. They all know who they are; each of them knows of my genuine gratitude to them. Without these people the book would not have been produced.

I do want to mention two people by name. With only three exceptions I have researched and written my own books without the help of an assistant. This book is one of the exceptions. Issam Smeir has been an incredible source of help, encouragement, and insight. He has helped find cases, critiqued my writing, given insightful counseling perspectives, and offered many valuable recommendations as this book manuscript has emerged. Then, once again, my wife Julie has walked with me through the long hours of producing a book. No words can express my gratitude to her for the many ways in which she has helped me through so many book projects, including this one.

Whenever I write a book I try to build a connection with the readers, but after the book goes to press there is no further communication with the readers except those that I might meet at a conference, talk with in a class, or communicate with on the Internet or through a radio interview. This time, to facilitate more contact with those of you who will read this book, a web site has been established at *www.garyrcollins.com*. In future years some people may read the prior sentence and discover that the web site is no longer active. (I can't promise to keep this going forever.) As this book goes to press, however, and for the foreseeable future, this web site will be a place for me to post additional materials that might be of interest to readers of this book and of *Christian Counseling: A Comprehensive Guide*. There will be opportunity there for readers to respond to the books, the cases, the author, and each other. My weekly newsletter on counseling and coaching will be posted on the web site (including information about how you can receive this personally) along with other postings that might appear from time to time in the future. Please keep in contact through the web site. And forgive me if I am unable to answer all your messages personally.

I began by stating that "counseling is an art; it is a skill, based on a body of knowledge and best learned by practice." Counseling also can be learned and counselors can grow by a careful consideration of case histories and how real-life counseling problems can be handled. It is my hope that God will give you rich growth experiences as you move through the pages that follow.

GARY R. COLLINS

## PART ONE

# Introductory Issues

# The Changes in Counseling

Counseling is about change, and counselors are agents of change. As their careers develop and their experiences increase, counselors become experts on change. They learn about change management, stimulating transformation in others and making modifications in themselves. Most Christ-followers know, as well, that the Christian life is about becoming different. Christian counselors seek to be God's instruments in bringing change to others who don't know how to change or don't have the energy to do things in new and different ways. This book is about change, and it starts with change in a Christian who, as these words are written, is in the process of becoming a Christian counselor.

Caroline is a young businesswoman who has decided to switch careers and become a professional Christian counselor. She has confidence that she would be effective as a counselor, she has done research about the training that would be required, and she has decided to apply for admission to a graduate school for Christian counselors. When her pastor learned about these plans, he became very critical. Over the years, Caroline has heard his sermons condemning "godless psychology" and the dangers of secular counseling. Initially Caroline agreed with these messages, but as she got older she grappled with the complexity of suffering and saw the power of Christian counseling in changing people's lives. She was not surprised when her desire to get counselor training led to a barrage of criticisms from the leaders of her church. Most of the arguments she had heard before:

- If people pray about their problems, God will take them away without secular humanistic psychology.
- Counseling is a tool that the devil and psychologists use to make people think they don't need God.
- The Bible says (in 2 Peter 1:3) that God has given us everything we need for living a godly life, so we don't need psychiatry, psychology, or counseling.
- When people bring their problems to the altar, there is healing, so they don't need counseling.
- The Bible is our guidebook for solving problems. The answer to every problem is in the Word of God, so man-made answers aren't needed and they don't work.
- Counselors turn people away from God, so Christians should avoid them.

## Discussion Questions

1. Suppose Caroline comes to you because she is feeling increased conflict about her changing beliefs with regards to counseling. As a counselor, how would help her through this conflict?

2. Assume that Caroline wants you to help her change the pastor's perspective about counseling. Based on what you have learned about change, what would you suggest that Caroline do or say so that a change in the pastor's attitude would be most likely to occur? What do you think are the chances that changes in the pastor's attitudes really will occur? Give reasons for your answer.

3. For Caroline, changing the pastor's perspective is important, but she also seeks guidance about whether she should change locations and start graduate education in counseling. As her counselor, what would you do to help her with these change issues?

## General Questions

1. As you reflect on your development as a counselor, what changes have you had in your own perspectives on the relationship between Christianity, counseling, and psychology?
2. How would you respond to each of the criticisms that Caroline's pastor raised?
3. How will you bring your Christian faith into your work as a counselor?
4. How will you answer the previous question if you are a Christian working in a secular setting where it is not permitted to mention Christian or other religious issues?

## Personal Reflection Questions

1. Who has criticized or raised objections about your decision to be a counselor? How have you responded to these objections? If they rise again, how will you respond, based on what you know about change?
2. In what specific ways are you changing because you are a counselor or becoming a counselor? Evaluate these changes.
3. List ways that you should change if you are to be a better counselor. How will you make these changes? Who will help? When will you get this help?

After prayerful consideration and a long conversation with the Christian counselor, Caroline decided to enroll in the counseling school. She has moved to a new community and has become involved with a church where the leadership has no criticisms of counseling or psychology. The longer she stays in her new environment the more she is convinced that she is entering the right career. She does well in her classes and is learning the basics of effective Christian counseling. She dreams of the day when she will have her own counseling practice where people will come to find help, guidance, and healing.

But the road forward is rarely easy for counselors in training. Even as they learn new facts and new skills, counselors learn about themselves and about making personal changes. As part of her training, Caroline was assigned to work in a residential treatment center for highly oppositional adolescents. At first she was enthusiastic about working with young people, but the first day at the treatment facility she was required to go through an all-day workshop on how to protect herself and manage the aggressive behaviors of her counselees. "These kids have a lot of pain," the instructor said. "They don't sit passively in a counselor's office, talking about their problems. Most of them don't want to be in counseling at all, and some of these people have been counseled so much that they know all the counselor's tricks. They do not know how to deal with emotion or frustration, so when they get angry or feel vulnerable, they respond with their fists. Not only can they be aggressive, but they also know how to manipulate and intimidate counselors." The instructor paused, smiled, and added, "You will learn here, but it may not be easy. So welcome to our treatment facility."

This is not what Caroline expected when she enrolled to be a counselor. She also did not expect that she might have to visit the parents and families of these adolescents, most often in their homes, sometimes in dangerous neighborhoods. This came as a surprise as she always assumed that counseling would take place in a comfortable office.

## Discussion Questions

1. As a counselor, what would you say to Caroline if she came to you and complained that the setting where she is working is not consistent with her personality and that it will do nothing to train her for her desired work in the office of a suburban counseling center? How could you help her to see the value of being in the setting where she is, at least temporarily?

2. Assuming that Caroline stays for the duration of her training in this new treatment facility, in what ways will she have to change? Be specific. How can she be helped to change in ways that will last?

3. One counselor who works in a similar facility read Caroline's story and said, "I was trained to do counseling in an office. When I got to this new setting, working with dysfunctional kids, I had to make a huge shift in my thinking and behavior." What kinds of shifts (changes) do you think Caroline will have to make?

## General Questions

1. Caroline is a Christian. What teachings from the Bible are relevant to Caroline's situation and to her need to adapt to the new setting?
2. What influences are making it difficult for Caroline to change as she adjusts to her new setting? Be specific in your answer. How could a counselor help Caroline deal with each of these changes?

## Personal Reflection Questions

1. What did you feel as you read each part of Caroline's story—the criticisms from her church and her need to make adjustments to her new work situation? Be honest. How would you respond and change if you were in either of these situations? Discuss your answers with a friend.
2. In your counseling training or career thus far, what are the biggest changes you have had to make? How have you handled these? How might you have handled them better?
3. What do you most fear about your training or career that is ahead? Is there some secret about yourself that you think might be discovered, some insecurity that might be uncovered, some mask that might be removed? If they persist and there is no change, how will each of these influences affect your counseling? Which of these should you start changing now? Who will help you make these changes? Be specific. When will you initiate these changes? If not now, why? If not until later, then when?
4. Caroline is discovering the changing world of Christian counseling. Undoubtedly most Christian counseling is done in places other than the comfortable counselor's office. What will this mean for your future and your career? (If you have a special interest in the changes in Christian counseling, skip ahead and read the final chapter of the *Christian Counseling* book for which this casebook is a companion.)

For a follow-up to the story of Caroline, please go to the Epilogue at the end of this book.

# The Counselor and Counseling

Counseling can be hard work. People often bring complex problems to their counselors, but there are few easy solutions. In turn, the counselors may bring their own needs, vulnerabilities, and unhealthy attitudes into counseling sessions. In addition, Christian leaders, especially pastors, often face unrealistic expectations from counselees and from people in the church. All of this can lead to the depression and burnout that are common among those who counsel. The following paragraphs, written in the counselor's own words, describe a youth pastor whose own actions created problems that almost destroyed his ministry.

"Rev. G is pastor of one of the largest and most dynamic evangelical churches in the state where he lives. Early one morning, this pastor called me (I am an experienced professional counselor and also a pastor) asking for guidance in dealing with the church's youth pastor. The youth leader, Sergio, is twenty-nine, married, the father of two children, and well liked, both by the teenagers in his youth group and by their parents. Several weeks before the pastor's call to the counselor, Sergio had met a young woman named Mariah who had visited the church a couple of times. When Sergio invited her to the youth group, Mariah said she was shy and didn't feel comfortable just going to the group without knowing anybody, so Sergio volunteered to pick her up from her house, take her to the church, and bring her home. After this happened several times, Mariah confessed that she was attracted to Sergio, and before long they were kissing and moving into more sexual touching. All of this led to a lot of guilt in Sergio, and finally he decided to tell his wife and the senior pastor. The wife forgave him, but the senior pastor asked Sergio to step down from his ministry role so he could 'work out the problems.' Sergio agreed but felt hopeless, embarrassed, weary, and convinced that he could never return to ministry. At Rev. G's suggestion, Sergio went to see a lay counselor in the church who made a suggestion that seemed unusual. 'Fire Sergio,' the counselor told the pastor. 'Then hire him to paint the church on the weekends. In this way he will experience the consequences of his sin by being humiliated, and the whole congregation will learn that God punishes even the pastors, so they should be aware of their conduct.' Rev. G was astonished at this advice and confused, so he called asking if I would meet with Sergio and his wife.

"When they walked into my office, Sergio looked distracted, restless, tired, and uncomfortable. The wife started by saying that they were desperate about the situation. She had forgiven her husband and wanted to move on with their lives and relationship, but she was tired and could not understand the state of her husband's mind. The pastor had forgiven Sergio and wanted to reinstate him. He had confessed to God but still felt hopeless and did not believe that he had been forgiven. At that point Sergio asked if his wife could leave the room because he wanted to tell me something more about the whole problem. His wife agreed to this and went out into the hall. I hesitated about continuing with this, but Sergio had made up his mind: he wanted to tell me details about what had happened. I said that it was not necessary to tell me everything that happened, but Sergio said he did not feel forgiven because he had not told anybody the whole truth. I decided to listen even though I knew this could fuel his desires to tell more and more. He told me about how many times they had kissed each other, where they kissed, what they did when they touched one another, and what they talked about. When he asked if he should tell his wife all these details, I suggested that this could stir up the issues further and feed her mind with exaggerated thoughts about what must have happened. He already had confessed to her, she had not asked for details, everybody had forgiven him, including God, and Sergio could be free to move forward. When he asked how I could be so sure God had forgiven him, I said, 'Because I am a professional Christian counselor and pastor, and I know that God has forgiven you.' I knew that this was a shallow answer, but it seemed to reassure him. In subsequent sessions, whenever the issue of details came up, I reassured him about God's forgiveness. His wife was concerned about this need to emphasize the details, but I told her not to worry because there were no new things. She accepted this and seemed to be at peace.

"Now, with the guilt largely out of the way, we had to address Sergio's depression. He thought the depression was God's punishment for the sin with Mariah, but I pointed out that God forgives a truly repentant person. Christ had taken the consequences of Sergio's sin to the cross, so the ongoing depression had to have a different origin. In counseling, Sergio described how his meetings with Mariah came at a time when he was feeling separation from God. This man's spiritual life had been under a lot of stress, and that probably contributed to the depression. In addition, we considered the self-punishment with which Sergio had been living and how that must have fed the depression too. Even so, I suspected that the depression had a different origin. I referred Sergio to a psychiatrist who prescribed Prozac. Then, while we waited for the Prozac to take its full effect (four to six weeks), I started to dig into his personality and background.

"Sergio was born in a large, middle- to low-income family. Surrounded by brothers and sisters, Sergio felt like an invisible kid that nobody noticed. He wasn't popular at school or church although he wasn't an outcast either. He was just one more kid. His dad used to work in another town, so the family would only see the father on weekends when he would spend most of his time building a larger house for the family. As a result, Sergio spent more time with his mother and grandparents. The grandfather was alcoholic, prone to violence when he was home, sometimes hitting Sergio's grandmother, mother, and even the children. So the family would hide when the grandfather was around, and sometimes they would play games like who could hide first. When Sergio was a teenager, he was more involved in the church youth group. After graduating from high school, he went to a Bible college and subsequently was invited to be youth pastor of the church where Rev. G was now the pastor. In his new role, Sergio suddenly shifted from being one member of the group to being its leader. Before, no one laughed at Sergio's jokes, but then everyone laughed at them. Sergio started preaching and doing counseling, and the young kids listened and respected him. He jumped from being a nobody to being the most popular person among the youth. When he came for counseling he was almost thirty and still struggling with his issues of identity. Who really was he? Was he the nobody or the youth pastor? The depression arose both from his guilt and from the ungrounded identity struggles. He was not happy about taking Prozac, or me telling him he was depressed, especially because the church leaders believed that depression is a sign of spiritual weakness."

This case is the true description of a depressed young man who comes for counseling. Assume the counselor is you, as you consider the following questions.

### Discussion Questions

1.  Lay counselors can and do have a significant positive ministry in church and other settings, but what is your opinion of the lay counselor who first saw Sergio and his wife? In what ways was the experienced counselor different? What counselor characteristics did the professional counselor demonstrate? Which of the counselors was better and why?
2.  Assume that Sergio asked you why he, a married man, had become involved with Mariah, who was young, single, not a Christian, and uncomfortable fitting in with the youth group. What do you think are the reasons for Sergio's behavior?
3.  How could a similar moral failure be prevented in the future? What might have prevented it from happening the first time?
4.  Why was guilt so engraved in Sergio's experience? Is there any relationship between the guilt he experienced and Sergio's background? What might be the impact of the alcoholic grandfather? What about the distant role of the father?
5.  Do you agree with the counselor that the wife did not need to hear details of Sergio's relationship with Mariah? What are reasons why the wife should not have had the details? Are there

reasons why she should hear the details? How would you have answered Sergio's question about whether to tell details to his wife? Give reasons for your answer.

6. The counselor felt that Sergio's identity confusion was partially the cause of his depression. How would you help Sergio clarify his identity and be more at peace with who he is?

## General Questions

1. How would you explain Sergio's ability to jump from dating this girl on Saturday night to preaching or teaching the youth group the following day?

2. What was uniquely Christian about the counselor's work? Where does the use of anti-depressant medication fit into your answer?

3. What would you do if Sergio agreed with the church leaders, concluded that depression is a sign of spiritual weakness, and refused to take anti-depressants?

4. The *Christian Counseling* book lists mistakes that counselors make. What mistakes, if any, did Sergio's counselor make?

5. In what ways, positive or negative, do you think the involvement with Mariah will affect Sergio's future ministry, marriage, and work as a youth counselor?

6. The first paragraph of this chapter mentions burnout. What is burnout, and what steps can you take to prevent it in you? Be specific.

## Personal Reflection Questions

1. What are your motives and needs for becoming a counselor? Write these in a journal, then discuss them with a trusted friend or counselor. How might these motives interfere with your effectiveness as a counselor?

2. Sergio got involved with a young woman in ways that created a number of problems and led to significant guilt. Be honest in answering this question: *What is there in your life that could make you vulnerable to sexual or other entanglements with a counselee?* In what specific ways can this be prevented in your counseling?

Discuss this with one other person who can be trusted. Usually it is best that private issues like this not be discussed in a class or large group.

For a follow-up to the story of Sergio, please go to the Epilogue at the end of the book.

# 3

# The Church and Counseling

Where do people go for help when they have a problem? When religion was more popular and prevalent than it is today, most people turned first to a priest, minister, or rabbi who gave pastoral counseling. Today pastoral counseling is still an important ministry of the church, although many pastors feel inadequate as counselors and some are uncomfortable in dealing with the personal problems of their parishioners and church visitors. Glen was interviewed for the case story that follows.

For ten years, Glen has been the lead pastor of a growing church. On his day off every Monday, this young pastor plays golf with a counselor friend, then they go for lunch. The two friends know each other well and enjoy getting together without any agenda or expectations. Sometimes Glen will talk about his church, his visions for the future, and his counseling.

"When I began at the church I had a policy of seeing counselees for no more than three sessions," Glen told his friend one Monday. "If they needed more, I would refer them to a professional counselor. To do that we needed to have a group of good counselors to whom we could make referrals so the pastors got to know the local mental health professionals. This worked well, but after a while I began to feel uncomfortable making referrals just as people were getting comfortable with me and beginning to make progress. I began to feel that the people in my church were being compartmentalized. The spiritual parts of their lives were being handled in the church while the personal and marital struggles were referred elsewhere. I began to wonder if I was making these referrals because I wanted to get the unhealthy people out of my office. Maybe these referrals were a way for me to escape responsibility for caring. I still make referrals, but more often I now see people longer and refer people less. Of course this means that I have to limit my counseling to fewer cases."

## Discussion Questions

1. Assume that you are Glen's counselor friend. Glen asks what you think about his counseling policy. What would you say? Give your reasons.

2. "Sometimes people are like sheep in the bushes," Glen suggested. "It takes more than two or three tries to get them untangled from the thorns. When they are untangled, they need help in finding direction." How would you respond to this picture?

3. "I have a young congregation," Glen continued. "Many of them are students, young parents, or people at the start of their careers. The older people who come to our church have a spiritual maturity, but they also seem to like the vitality and enthusiasm of the younger church attendees. I think we need to show all of our people that the church is not called to deny or to push away individuals who are different from the rest of us or unhealthy." What could Glen do to communicate this message to his church members? Give practical answers.

This conversation led Glen to start talking about homeless people who come to his church, often wanting money or other forms of practical help. Recently a disheveled couple appeared. They had been sleeping in a vacant lot near the church because they had no place to stay. The woman was pregnant, the couple did not have any money, and they appeared to have dire needs. Several weeks later a middle-aged woman appeared with her daughter. They had been sleeping in the woman's car, but when the girl's school discovered this, they were told that if this continued the couple would be reported to the state and the daughter probably would be taken to a foster home. The woman asked the church for help. At about this same time a forty-five-year-old man asked if he could sleep every night in his car in the church parking lot. He had a job that did not pay well, so he had no home. He did have some paranoia, however, fearing that the church would kick him off the property. All three of these—the couple, the woman and daughter, and the single man—wanted money, food, and a place to stay. Cases like these were relatively common for Glen, but they tended to wear him down. If he asked how to handle these kinds of cases, what would you tell him?

In reflecting on his counseling ministry, Glen made two interesting comments. "I think we need to be equipped and resourced," he said. "We need to work with other churches—even if we disagree with their theologies—with the village where we live, and with community agencies, so that all of us can take responsibility to give help. It is hard to talk to people about Jesus when they are hungry, cold, and worried. Most of the local religious leaders recognize this, and now we have a directory of local resources that we can consult in times of need." In Glen's community all these groups got together and formed what they call TAP—Temporary Assistance Program. Each of the churches and some community groups give money to a fund that can provide short-term housing, food, or other services. Any pastor can give a coupon to somebody in need. He or she then takes this to the police station where there is a check on the help seeker's identity and control lest the same people go from church to church looking for handouts. With police approval, the immediate needs are met until longer-term needs can be dealt with.

Glen also had a comment about counseling. "I learned in seminary about the importance of showing compassion and genuine care. That is important, but I think admonition is of equal importance. Sometime people need to be admonished and challenged, even as they need to be encouraged."

## Discussion Questions

1. Look up Colossians 1:28. The *New International Version* says "We proclaim him (Christ), admonishing and teaching everyone

with all wisdom." What is the place of admonishing people, teaching them, and giving encouragement?

2. What would you say if Glen asked how you would have helped the couple, the woman and her daughter, and the homeless man?

3. How would you advise Glen to help the people in his congregation understand the importance of helping the homeless in their community?

4. Discuss the TAP program. Would this work in your community? How could it be developed where you live? What are its advantages and disadvantages?

## General Questions

1. As a counselor, what is your opinion on the emergent/missional church? What experiences have you had with these churches? What has the emergent church taught you about counseling? What can it teach you, even if you do not agree with its methods or goals?

2. Can you name characteristics that distinguish traditional, pragmatic, and emergent churches? Can you think of examples of each in your community? How might counseling be done in each of these churches?

3. Many people are interested in spirituality but not in the church or in religion. How can Christian counselors help people in this group?

## Personal Reflection Questions

1. How does spiritual formation relate to your work as a counselor?

2. Regardless of your theological position, how does your counseling relate both to the local church and to the field of professional counseling? Look at the section on church-psychology collaboration in the *Christian Counseling* book. How does this relate to your work as a counselor now? How will it relate to your work as a counselor in the future?

3. Be honest. What is your opinion of the church? How will this relate to your work as a counselor?

4. Would you fit in an emergent church? Why or why not?

For a follow-up to the story of Pastor Glen, please go to the Epilogue at the end of the book.

# The Community and Counseling

When you think of counseling, what comes to mind? For many counseling students and professionals, counseling implies one or more face-to-face conversations in an office and between a person with a problem and another person who is there to help solve the problem. In reality it may be that most counseling occurs far from any office setting—in homes, in churches, on the streets, at the sites of tragedy or disaster, in hospital rooms, or in jails. In spite of the image to the contrary, it may be that most counselors don't even have offices. They go to where the people are and do counseling in the community.

Community Counseling Services (CCS) is a Christian agency that exists to meet the psychological, spiritual, and tangible needs of people living in a medium-sized city that once was thriving but that now appears to be dying because of a downturn in the local economy. CCS offers a variety of services. These include group counseling and other assistance for mothers identified by Child Protective Services as having abused or neglected their children. Led by two counselors, the Mothers' Group meets every week to give social support, encouragement, and guidance. Most of these women have little support from others, and many are overwhelmed by the challenges of trying to survive while they care for their kids. There are meals at every meeting, and volunteers provide childcare so the mothers can focus their attention on the group. (The children eat with the moms and counselors, then play in another room with babysitters while the meeting takes place.) To keep the mothers involved and coming, volunteers provide transportation to and from the meeting. This is because it is a challenge for each mother to round up several kids, find the bus fare, and take public transportation every week.

In the first half of the weekly meetings, the mothers are encouraged to share about their stresses, interactions with their children, and occasional victories. The second half of the meeting is structured and focuses on things like self-care, parenting techniques, and community resources. These include job training programs, licensed daycare facilities, and church activities such as literacy programs, after-school programs for children, Bible studies, and discipleship groups. Some churches have an "Adopt a Family" program in which church members mentor families involved in the Mothers' Group.

Yvette is a twenty-year-old single mom who attends the Mothers' Group. She came from a broken home, the first child of her unmarried mother, who was only seventeen when Yvette was born. Eventually five other children were born, but only two had the same father.

Yvette hasn't seen her father since she was two, and he never has supported her financially or emotionally. As she tried to raise her six children, Yvette's mother struggled with depression and often would withdraw from her family and from the world. When Yvette was eight years old, her mother began to use heroin as a way of coping. As a result, Yvette and her five younger siblings pretty much were left to fend for themselves.

Not many years later, Yvette herself got pregnant at the age of fourteen, and now she has four children of her own, all under the age of five. She was happy when she found out she was pregnant the first time. For most of her life she had struggled with loneliness and assumed that a baby would ease her emptiness. For most of her teenage years, however, Yvette has been trying to make a better life for herself and her children, but she has done so with little help. About two years ago, she began her own journey with depression.

She was determined not to turn to drugs like her mother had, but she has had few coping skills and no reliable person in her life. By the time she was eighteen, Yvette looked like she was forty-five. She was often sick and always stressed as she tried to raise her four kids and work at a part-time job that only paid a minimum wage. Yvette's ability to handle the typical demands of children diminished over time.

As her patience decreased, her yelling increased. As her yelling increased, her children's negative behaviors escalated. Soon, her children were out of control, and Yvette didn't know what to do. Eventually, what began as physical discipline turned into physical abuse. Yvette began to beat the children into compliance.

One day the school nurse noticed bruises on one child and called Child Protective Services. The caseworker assigned to the family referred Yvette to the Mothers' Group. At first, Yvette felt uncomfortable in the group and resisted going. She was embarrassed to have others know about her struggles and felt awkward when people tried to get to know her. She wasn't used to accepting help and certainly wasn't accustomed to other people trying to be helpful. Almost a year passed before she was able to trust some of the others in the Mothers' Group. Once she began to trust, however, she began to open herself up to other opportunities. She got involved with a Women's Bible Study at the partnering church and signed up for a mentor family. Both have had a tremendous impact on her life, and recently she even has been considering baptism.

## Discussion Questions

1. Give reasons why the Mothers' Group and CCS have been able to meet Yvette's needs better than one-to-one counseling in a formal office setting.
2. Most of Yvette's counseling has come from the group and from the church mentor family. How might individual counseling supplement this community form of treatment?
3. Working within a community requires partnerships and cooperation between individual counselors and others. With whom did the caseworker form partnerships? What other community resources might have been tapped by the caseworker or the counselors who lead the Mothers' Group?

## General Questions

1. In what ways has Yvette been like her mother? In what ways is Yvette different? If you were working with Yvette, what would you do to prevent the same dysfunctional patterns (teenage preg-

nancies, intense poverty, feelings of being overwhelmed, inability to cope, for example) from being repeated in Yvette's children?

2. Think of the environment where you work as a counselor or where you hope to work. In what ways can community resources make your counseling more effective in the place where you might do counseling? What community resources would be available?

3. Yvette has found help in a local church. How might your church become involved in helping people like Yvette? Realistically, do you think this would happen? What are the obstacles that might prevent your church's involvement?

## Personal Reflection Questions

1. Imagine that you are offered a job working in a place like CCS. Assuming that the pay and other benefits are good, would you accept such a job? Why or why not? What would make you uncomfortable working with people like Yvette or the women in her group?

2. If you would feel uncomfortable in working with poor or dysfunctional people like Yvette, give some personal thought to your reasons why. Certainly not everybody works well in an environment like CCS, but take some time to ponder the reasons for your resistance in light of Jesus' frequent teaching about caring for the poor. Write down your thoughts in a journal and consider sharing them with a person you can trust.

3. Assume that your church focuses on evangelism or discipleship but overlooks the needs of people in the community, including nonbelievers. What gives the church a biblical justification for ignoring community care-giving? What does the Scripture say about involvement with the community's needs? Ask God to guide as you consider these issues. Would you agree that these are spiritual as well as personal reflection issues?

4. In what practical ways will you change as a result of your personal reflections on this chapter? If you do not plan to change in any way, write down your reasons for this decision.

For a follow-up to the story of Yvette, please go to the Epilogue at the end of the book.

# The Core of Counseling

The introduction to this book began with the statement that counseling is an art. Every case is like a painting of people with problems that have different forms, colors, and shades of gray. Counselors get the painting tools in their training programs, but they rarely have all the answers for the uniquely colored needs, questions, and expectations people bring for counseling. Because of this, counselors must rely on the guidance of the Holy Spirit to give creative, inspired direction. The following case is told by a missionary counselor who has professional training and who works mostly with church leaders who are native to the country where he lives. On occasion, this counselor works with other missionaries who paint their own word pictures of strain and pressure. Here is the counselor's story:

"Loneliness is a major issue for many missionaries. Through technology it is easy to be in contact with people at home and with other missionaries, but it can be difficult to find good friends with whom one can be accountable. My family and I were facing this missionary loneliness ourselves when a new missionary family arrived in our community and we became really good friends. Their call was to plant churches; my ministry was to counsel local church leaders. We had good times as families, but always I felt that something was missing in our friendship. We could not go beyond a limit of superficiality that the new couple set, so we just respected this. Soon, they were transferred to a city four hundred miles north of where we were living.

"Months later, we decided to get together as families for a brief vacation. During the first days together everyone had a great time, but the husband seemed sad and his wife appeared to be distant. On the day we were leaving, he talked to me and said he had a small problem that few people knew about although his wife did know. I wasn't sure if it was wise for us to talk about this on the day we were leaving. Also, I wondered if I was the right person to listen to him since we were good friends. In my counselor training classes I had learned that a counselor should not have dual relationships with the counselee. Was it right for me to be his counselor when I was his friend? Sometimes in real-life situations, however, things are different from what we discuss in graduate school. What was I to do as my friend started sharing? I knew that he lived in a place where there were no other Christian counselors. So I just listened.

"Bob, the missionary, was twenty-eight years old at the time, and for ten years he had been hooked on pornography. Maybe Bob thought that he could free himself from this addiction if he became a missionary and moved far from home, but he soon discovered that the Internet and other technology could give him easy access to pornography wherever he was living. For Bob, his computer and the local television networks were like living with a pile of pornographic magazines on the nightstand near his bed. A fresh supply of sexual stimulation was always available, and he could hide the evidence with one click on his computer keyboard if his wife or anybody else walked into the room. On the day when our families were leaving, Bob and his wife had had a big fight. She had caught him masturbating while watching pornography on television. He said that he felt embarrassed and hopeless about ever getting free of his addiction and the compulsive masturbation that went with it.

"Bob decided to open up to me because his wife told him that they could not continue in the ministry, living this kind of life. He agreed but told me that he couldn't control his actions. Then he started asking all kinds of questions that counselors can't always answer. 'Can you help me?' 'What's wrong with me?' 'Do I have hope?' 'What should I do?' 'Should I resign from the mission?' 'What will I tell my family and the people in my church back home if I resign?' I felt the pressure to come up with answers to his questions, but I had no idea what to tell him, especially when there was no time to talk further.

He said that he had struggled with the problem for years, prayed about it, repented many times, fasted, and begged God to take it away, but nothing had worked. At one time he got enough courage to tell a pastor about the problem, and the pastor concluded that Bob probably was demon-possessed. The pastor said that Satan had strongholds in Bob's life and that he needed to be liberated. So, the church elders had a special session to free him from this demon. Shortly after the session, he was back to the web, feeling the rush to return to the porn. As he prepared to leave on the day that we talked, he told me in a dejected way that he had tried everything and nothing seemed to work.

"We agreed to keep in contact by telephone and to find a way for us to meet again as soon as we could. I did not ask him to stop masturbating or watching porn, but I encouraged him to keep a journal about his activities. He agreed to record his temptations every day. At the end of the day he would give a number to each day. Number one meant that there were no temptations that day. Number two meant 'I felt tempted, I wanted to act out, and even took some steps to fall, but I controlled myself and did not go any further.' Numbers three and four indicated progressive involvement, and number five meant that he watched pornography and masturbated while doing so. He agreed to send an email to me giving a report at the end of each day. Bob agreed, as well, that he would turn around his computer so the screen was visible from the door to his office and that he would always leave the door open. That would mean that his wife or anybody else who walked past his room could see what was on the computer screen.

"As planned, we kept in touch through email messages and phone calls, then one month later we met again. The journal had helped Bob monitor the circumstances that could lead to temptation, and this also gave him encouragement when he could see that there were days when he was not tempted and days when he was tempted but did not fall. I knew, however, that the record keeping was only a temporary method that could lose its power after a couple of months. We needed to look at issues that might be causing Bob's problem.

"Bob's parents were missionaries who sent him to a boarding school when he was only seven. The children slept in large rooms where boys of all ages were in one room and the girls were in another. There were missionaries who supervised the children, but they kept aloof and showed no evidences of love for the often lonely and sad kids who were at the school. When his parents came to visit or when Bob went on vacation, he wanted to tell his parents how unhappy he was, but the boarding school leaders had instructed the children to always appear happy when they were with their parents. The children were told that if they complained or appeared unhappy the parents would be worried and not able to do their missionary work. Satan would use the children's sad looks to hurt the parents, and maybe they even would have to stop their work and go home because the children were not happy.

"Bob learned to keep his emotions hidden, even when a school maintenance worker started abusing him sexually at the age of twelve. This abuse continued for two years until the worker was fired from his job because of laziness. Bob never told anyone about the pain inside, about the efforts to hide his feelings, about the shame he had felt at the boarding school. Then, fifteen years later he told me, his counselor. Bob had never dared to get close to people before, not even to his wife. Instead he found intimacy with the images on the computer or television screen. They were images that he could control, accompanied by feelings of pleasure that he could generate for himself without being hurt. We looked at his journal and were able to see that whenever Bob felt lonely, out of control, starved for intimacy, or depressed, he would feel a rush of adrenaline pushing him to the pornographic images. In talking with me, Bob had found an accountability partner who helped him understand and get control of his emotions and his addiction. He also found acceptance and a healthy, nonsexual intimacy with a friend who did not condemn him, like he had condemned himself, and did not jump to the conclusion that Bob was demon-possessed."

### Discussion Questions

1. The missionary counselor who told this story is Bob's friend. Do you think a friend can really be an effective counselor, even in unusual circumstances? Is it ethical for a friend to do counseling with a friend? Do unusual circumstances make this acceptable? What would you have done? Give reasons for your answer.

2. Read over the section on the goals of counseling in the *Christ-ian Counseling* book. What goals would apply to the case of Bob? Why would some of the others not be good goals?
3. What counseling skills would you need to counsel Bob?
4. What do you think might be the real causes of his porno-graphic addiction? Would you suggest any causes other than those that Bob's counselor suggested?
5. Bob's counselor used some homework assignments. What were these? What other homework might the counselor have given Bob? Why would these be effective?

## General Questions

1. Bob described the pastor's efforts to exorcise demons. Based on your understanding of Scripture, do you think demons may be involved in Bob's addiction? Give reasons for your answer. If demons are involved, then why did the exorcism not free Bob from his addictive behavior?
2. Review the process of counseling as outlined in the *Christian Counseling* book. What process did Bob's counselor use? Why was this effective?
3. Would group counseling have been helpful for Bob? Why or why not?

## Personal Reflection Questions

1. Later in this book we will discuss issues like sexual addiction and masturbation. In this chapter, however, consider the process of counseling as a whole. If Bob had told you about his problem, what would have made you feel overwhelmed per-sonally? Give reasons for this. How can you counsel concern-ing difficult problems without being overwhelmed?
2. The counselor began his report by stating that he had been feeling lonely on the mission field and that Bob had felt lonely too. Assume that the counselor also had a problem with sexual addiction. How would this have influenced the counseling?
3. List the problem areas in your life that would hinder you from counseling others who have similar problems. For example, if

you have a marriage problem, it may not be wise for you to counsel others who have a marriage problem. Who can you talk to about the problem areas in your life that could hinder your counseling? When will you talk to another person about these problem areas? If you ignore these personal areas, how could your counseling effectiveness be hindered and your counselees even be harmed?

For a follow-up to the story of Bob, please go to the Epilogue at the end of the book.

# Legal, Ethical, and Moral Issues in Christian Counseling

Sometimes legal, ethical, or moral issues arise in counseling without warning. In the case of Matt, the counselor was presented with a dilemma after the counseling had been progressing well. Here is the story, written in the counselor's own words.

"Matt came for counseling because of typical depressive symptoms. He had a general sense of hopelessness about the future, difficulty concentrating, problems with appetite and sleeping, low motivation, and some thoughts about suicide. Initially, Matt spoke quite eloquently about the root of his depression, which he believed centered on problems in the workplace, low self-esteem, and an intense fear of interpersonal rejection. It wasn't until the fourth session that he very casually mentioned that he had struggled for years to be honest with people about 'who he really was' and that he had only recently been able to subscribe to *The Advocate*, a national gay and lesbian newspaper. I racked my brain to remember our conversation in the initial session about his dating life. He had mentioned only that he didn't date much and that he felt no one would find him attractive. Even though I was a bit unsure of Matt's sexual orientation based on the vague statements he had made, I decided I needed to ask him directly whether he was gay. It took him sixty seconds or so to answer the question directly, and he still couldn't bring himself to say the words 'I'm gay.' During the rest of that fourth session, Matt talked about how he was convinced that his depression ultimately was driven by his inability to 'come out' and admit his homosexuality to his friends and family. At the end of the session, he asked if I could help him learn more about how to embrace his sexual orientation and to be more comfortable in the gay culture in general and with gay relationships in particular.

"Next session, Matt reported that he had known since he was eleven that he was 'different.' Although he never acted on any sexual feeling with another person until he was in college, he did have issues surrounding compulsive masturbation and pornography that began when he was around age fifteen and had continued ever since. Matt told me on several occasions that he had never been sexually abused as a child.

"When asked about his family, the counselee reported that he had fought terribly with his parents when he was an adolescent. His father was a very likable fellow who was a successful politician, but he was often absent from the home. The counselee reported that he now had a positive relationship with his father, but that it had been very shallow during the growing-up years. Matt's relationship with his mother was different. She was overbearing and controlling and had been overprotective of the counselee throughout his childhood. Matt and his mother argued intensely when he was in adolescence, and they still disagreed strongly even over very small matters.

"The parents were an extremely religious couple that had raised their children in a mainline Christian denomination. Matt reported that he sometimes still went to church, and that his church had recently started to ordain homosexuals to the ministry."

### Ethical Dilemmas

"I am a Christian psychologist but the name of my practice is not overtly religious. I market myself to doctors in my area who are not believers, and they send me many of their patients who are looking for a good psychologist, not necessarily a good Christian counselor. One of these doctors referred Matt to me, and he never requested counseling that was from a faith base. I struggled with helping Matt engage a lifestyle that I thought was destructive and perhaps fueling his depression. At the same time I felt uncomfortable imposing my evangelical beliefs on someone who had not asked for Christian counseling. I questioned whether it was OK for me to counsel Matt in view of our very different perspectives on the gay lifestyle. This did not feel right for me as a believer.

"Another ethical concern related to matters of faith in general. If I did decide to counsel Matt, what would I do with the fact that his faith tradition openly accepted homosexuals, and mine didn't? Was it ethical for me to impose my view of Scripture on Matt considering he never asked for Christian counseling in the first place? I also struggled with the question of whether I could work with Matt to help him embrace his new gay relationships even as I stayed true to my own convictions.

"As I thought over these questions, I became convinced that I probably was not the best counselor for Matt. But then it hit me. If I were to refer Matt to another counselor after we had completed several sessions and had built a solid therapeutic relationships, that would more than likely make him feel rejected as a person. Since interpersonal rejection was one of his main issues, would referring Matt make me break my ethical and moral duty to 'do no harm'? Also, it was quite possible that since Matt's depression had lifted a bit in the last month or two, the possibility of suicide might be greater. He now had more energy, and referring him would confirm his belief that he was unlovable and worthless because he would think that 'Even the counselor doesn't like me.'"

## Discussion Questions

1. If you were the counselor, what would you do? Why?
2. The counselor presents two options as he tells his story: (a) make a referral to some other counselor who would be more comfortable helping Matt be more open and accepting of his homosexuality, or (b) continue counseling Matt so that he could reach his desired goals with the present counselor's help. What other options are available? How would each of the options have potential to violate the counselor's legal and ethical responsibilities as a mental health professional? How would each option violate this counselor's personal, moral, spiritual, and/or worldview values?
3. How would each of the options help or hinder Matt's recovery and future well-being?

4. How would you answer the previous questions if you worked in a church setting or Christian counseling clinic? How would you answer if you worked in a secular setting?

5. If you chose not to help Matt embrace his new lifestyle, would you be guilty of showing discrimination based on a gender-orientation bias?

6. Assume that you decide to make the referral to another counselor. How would you present this to Matt, without stimulating the idea that "even my counselor doesn't like me"? How would you explain this to the referring physician? How would this impact your practice if the referring doctors concluded that your bias was harming the patients they referred?

## General Questions

1. Read this quotation from the *Christian Counseling* book: "Counselors sincerely seek what is best for each counselee's welfare. We do not attempt to manipulate, meddle in the counselee's life, ask questions to satisfy our own curiosity, or use counselees to meet our own needs. As servants of God, each counselor has a responsibility to live, act, and counsel in accordance with scriptural principles. As employees, counselors attempt to fulfill their responsibilities and perform duties faithfully and competently. As citizens and members of society, counselors obey the laws, submit to governmental authorities, and contribute to the good of the culture." How would this apply to Matt's counselor?

2. Reflecting on all of the prior questions, how does your commitment as a Christian influence your decision? Be specific. How *should* your commitment as a Christian have an influence?

## Personal Reflection Questions

1. The *Christian Counseling* book suggests that all people have a worldview that influences their behavior, perceptions, and moral decisions whether or not they recognize this consciously. Your worldview influences how you think and how you counsel even if you have never given your worldview any thought.

Write out your worldview on paper. Show this to somebody you trust and discuss your beliefs about the world together.

2.  Usually our behavior, interactions with others, patterns of spending money, choice of friends, lifestyle, and similar issues are a reflection of our worldviews. What is the evidence that what you have written in response to the previous question really is your worldview?

3.  Do you think your worldview could change? How would you like it to be different? How could you change it?

4.  How would your own sexuality influence your work with Matt? Would you be attracted to him and his sexual orientation, repulsed by his sexual orientation, tempted to ask questions to satisfy your own curiosity? Take time to consider these questions. Discuss them with a trusted friend or counselor if one is available. Recognize that Matt's struggle could arouse similar struggles that you, the counselor, might or should be facing honestly.

5.  What limits do you have in your own life to protect yourself against sexual immorality in your counseling and other relationships? Table 6–2 in *Christian Counseling* can help you answer this question. If you have no clear limits, what limits and guidelines do you need to have in place? When will you get these limits established? Be specific.

For a follow-up to the story of Matt, please go to the Epilogue at the end of the book.

# 7

# Multicultural Issues
# in Christian Counseling

This is one of several chapters that include two case stories. The first concerns a Spanish-speaking Hispanic family that lives in a community where most people are not Hispanic. The second story concerns recent refugees from Liberia who are trying to get settled in a large American city. Each family saw the same counselor. As you will discover, each family brought a unique cultural perspective into the counseling relationship.

## CASE STORY 1—The Rodriguez Family

Mr. and Mrs. Rodriguez were referred for counseling by a local community agency. The couple is having difficulty in managing their three children but especially their fourteen-year-old son, Jorge. According to the school, Jorge is an intelligent young man who speaks very good English, even though Spanish is spoken at home. He is a good athlete and has the ability to be a good student, but he is discourteous, rebellious, and disruptive in class. On many days he refuses to go to school, he rarely does his homework, and he seems to have an uncanny ability to annoy his classmates. At home he shows a variety of behavior problems that put him in conflict with his parents, his siblings, and sometimes the neighbors. The school does not know how to deal with Jorge, and the parents feel helpless in the face of his disruptive behavior.

The parents came together for the first counseling session, but they appeared to be distant, angry, and unable to work together. They both spoke good English, but their counselor had difficulty connecting with them and building rapport. When she commented that there appeared to be tension between them, they both denied this strongly and quickly changed the subject. There seemed to be little structure in the home, and whenever the counselor said anything about Jorge's problems, Mr. Rodriguez minimized the issue and insisted that the boy was fine.

Next session the mother came alone. She was very willing to talk about her son's problems, but when the counselor asked about the husband, Mrs. Rodriguez stated that he had refused to come. He told his wife to tell the counselor that he was busy doing other important things in life such as working. The wife commented that her husband was angry with her for seeking help. He did not think that there was anything wrong with the son except that he was ill-mannered and that this was the mother's fault. The father apparently thought that he was a good parent but raising the children was his wife's responsibility and something that she needed to handle. Once she had begun talking about her life at home, Mrs. Rodriguez went on to complain about her husband's outbursts of anger, his lack of interest in her or her family, and his consistent absence from the home so he could spend time with his friends.

## Discussion Questions

1. Sensing that this might be a long-term case, the counselor decided to make a referral and sent the Rodriguez family to you. Mrs. Rodriguez came to the first session without her husband and asked you to call him and ask him to come to the counseling sessions with her. How would you respond to this request? Would you call him? Give your reasons.

2. Since you have never met Mr. Rodriguez, how would you build rapport with him and get his cooperation?

3. What cultural issues and expectations could be relevant in your understanding of this family and in your attempts to help them? In what ways might cultural issues be involved in Mr. Rodriguez's unwillingness to come for counseling?

4. How would you involve Jorge in the counseling? Would you see him alone, with his parents, or not at all? Would you involve the other children? Give reasons for your answers.

5. What would be your counseling goals and methods in working with this family? How would these goals and methods be different if you were/are Hispanic and decided to counsel the family using the Spanish language?

## General Questions

1. What would you do if Mr. Rodriguez refused to come for counseling?
2. How would you deal with the husband's view that Jorge is fine and that solving the boy's problems is the wife's responsibility?
3. In what ways would your perspective as a Christian influence the ways in which you would work with this family?

## Personal Reflection Questions

Please see the end of this chapter for personal reflection questions.

## CASE STORY 2—Hamadi's Family

A refugee resettlement agency referred this family for counseling. The husband, Hamadi; his wife of twenty years, Amira; and their nine children recently had moved to the United States from Liberia through the refugee resettlement program. The purpose for the referral was to help this family adjust to life in a country where they are minorities and where life is so different from their country of origin. The counseling agency to which they were referred is Christian and supported by various local churches. The referring agency is aware of this, but since the counselors are known to be competent and since they do not attempt to proselytize, refugees are referred regardless of their beliefs and religious practices. Hamadi's family is Muslim. The family members practice and perform daily prayers and attend a nearby mosque.

Three years after their arrival, and while the counseling was in progress (and going well), Hamadi's second wife, Salima, arrived in the United States through the same program. She had three sons of her own whom Hamadi had fathered. Salima moved into an apartment in the same complex where her husband, Hamadi, lives with

Amira and the children. With the blessing of the leader of the mosque, Hamadi committed to taking care of his two households despite the financial and other pressures that this created. The women maintained separate households, and Hamadi treated both wives equally, including regular sexual relations with both. Within a few months after Salima's arrival, however, tension began to build between the two wives. Amira started feeling overwhelmed as Salima and her children became increasingly dependent. Amira began to feel that in addition to her own children she had three additional children to care for. Hamadi too was getting increasingly frustrated with the new arrangement. Salima did not seem to be herself anymore. She was sad and spent most of her time sleeping. When Hamadi would argue with her about the situation, she would become violent. At one point, the police got involved when a neighbor called for help after hearing noises of fighting coming from Hamadi's apartment. Salima resisted having sex with her husband, but she nevertheless became pregnant. Hamadi considered divorce, but according to Islamic law this would be impossible while the wife was pregnant.

Hamadi brought all of this to the counseling center, reporting that both households were in turmoil. Clearly he was overwhelmed with his circumstances. He wanted to be morally upright and do the right thing, but he had no idea what action to take. He cared for his wives and his children, but he was angry because they did not get along and confused about Salima's apparent withdrawal and abdication of her responsibilities as a mother.

With the husband's approval and encouragement, the counselor visited Salima in her apartment where they were able to talk together in Arabic. Salima described some of her difficulties in adjusting to her new circumstances in America. Prior to her arrival she had lived in a refugee camp where she had been raped. Because of her past traumatic experiences, she reported that upsetting memories usually were triggered if she saw anything violent on television or if she smelled anything that might be related to the smell of fire. Neighbors in the area noticed that Salima had a very hard time tolerating any noise. Several of them stated that they had stopped inviting her to their social gatherings or to public places because she always complained of having a severe headache. These symptoms added to Salima's social isolation from her family and friends. She confided that because of the rape, having sex with her husband triggered nightmares and upsetting memories, but she had not told any of this to Hamadi and did not know how to tell him that she had been abused sexually.

## Discussion Questions

1. If you had not recognized this before, perhaps these two cases make it clearer that counseling with multicultural issues can be complex and difficult. Suppose Hamadi and his wives were referred to you for counseling and assume that no other counselor is available. What would you do? Where would you start in your work with this family? Give reasons for your decision.

2. Hamadi is overwhelmed with his circumstances and not sure what to do. What would be your goals in working with him and his family? What methods might you use? Give reasons for your answer.

3. What cultural issues will you need to keep in mind as you work with this family?

4. What will you do if Hamadi does not agree with your goals or methods?

5. You will notice that the counselor went to the home of Salima and spoke with her in Arabic. (The counselor is a Christian from a Middle Eastern country.) Does this qualify as an indigenous method? What ethical issues, if any, does this violate?

6. Amira is angry both at herself for taking on the extra responsibility of caring for Salima's children and at Salima, who appears to have given up responsibility for her children. In Muslim culture, the second wife is expected to help the first wife, but here the roles have been reversed. How would you counsel Amira?

7. Salima is described as emotionally unavailable, traumatized, sad, confused, and unable to cope. She feels helpless, overwhelmed, fearful of sex, and bothered by nightmares. How would you help this woman who has had a variety of traumatic experiences and serious problems?

8. How can you help her tell the husband about being raped?

9. What are practical ways in which you can restore harmony between Hamadi and Amira? How can you help the relation-

ship between Hamadi and Salima? Are there ways to build a better relationship between Salima and Amira?

10. What is the place of your Christian beliefs, commitment, and methods in working with this Muslim family?

## General Questions

1. Do you have any legal responsibility in working with a polygamous family like this one? The second wife in these situations often tells the authorities that her husband has died and that she is a widow. Most of the neighbors still do not know that Salima is Hamadi's second wife.

2. The *Christian Counseling* book summarizes some stages of cultural adaptation. How do these apply to Hamadi and his families?

3. What might be the advantages and disadvantages of having both a male and a female counselor who could work jointly with these people?

4. You will notice that the case makes very little mention of the children. What would you want to know about them? Why would you want to know this? Would you try to involve them with the counseling? Why or why not?

5. In what ways could Christian principles and biblical truths help this family? In what ways could the application of these Christian principles further disrupt and overwhelm these people? Be specific.

6. Is it possible for you as a follower of Christ to do Christian counseling with a Muslim family? How could this be done?

7. Remember the setting for this counseling. The family has been referred by a government agency that does not expect you to convert these people to become Christ followers. You are a Christian. Would you continue to work with these people? Give reasons for your answer. There are no other local agencies working to help refugees get settled. In what ways does that influence your decision?

8. Discuss the role of God in your work with this family.

**Personal Reflection Questions**

1. What is your attitude toward working with people who are culturally different from you? Write your honest response in a journal. Some people connect very well cross-culturally, but others do not. What about you? With whom can you discuss this?
2. How can you build multicultural competence in yourself? Be specific. When will you start doing this? Who will hold you accountable?
3. Are there some cross-cultural situations where you could be more effective than others? What are these situations? Why are some easier or more appropriate for you than others?

For a follow-up to the stories of the Rodriguez family and of Hamadi, Amira, and Salima, please go to the Epilogue at the end of the book.

PART TWO

# Prominent Issues

# 8

# Depression

Depression has been called "the number one cause of disability world-wide." It is the most common disorder experienced by people who see mental health professionals, and it may be the most common problem in mental health workers themselves. At times almost everybody gets depressed. This depression may be mild and temporary, but for some people depression is like a heavy weight that pulls them down and puts a cloud over every corner of their lives. Consider Jennie.

She was described by her counselor as "one of the most depressed people that I have ever seen in private practice." It was a major effort for her to get to the counselor's office, and when she arrived she appeared to have no energy and no ability to concentrate, in part because she had gone night after night with little or no sleep. She showed no emotion, no motivation to do anything, no hope about the future. The counselor wondered if she might be a person with "treatment-resistant depression."

Jennie had not always been this way, but the roots of her depression appeared to have come early and been cultivated in her family. Jennie's father was a retired military officer who was rigid, hard to please, bound to rules, and inclined to see every issue in terms of black or white. Jennie could never please him. No matter how hard she tried, he would point out something that could have been done better. The mother appeared to have no power in the family. Passively, she accepted her husband's dominance and did nothing to protect her daughter. In contrast to Jennie, her brother was a party-goer who drank a lot and sometimes got into trouble. Instead of being criticized, the brother was continually affirmed by the father, who made excuses and appeared to think that his son could do no wrong. The family had no Christian background, and on the rare occasions when they went to church they tended be critical of the clergy, the service, and the people there, who were dismissed as stuffy members of a suburban social club.

Jennie was in her late twenties when she started college, and she did very well. She was a straight-A student who was witty, articulate, intelligent, and charming. She supported herself as a bartender and seemed to do well in everything she tried. Deep within, however, Jennie felt that nothing she did was good enough. She was not doing enough, making enough difference, or earning enough money. She never allowed herself to succeed but repeatedly sabotaged her efforts instead. A few weeks before graduation, she dropped out of the university and had to finish later. Shortly before she was scheduled to start graduate school, she changed her mind and applied to a different program. When she got halfway through her MA training, she developed a seizure disorder that squelched her graduate school career. The seizures appeared to have a legitimate medical basis, but Jennie latched onto this condition, seemed to delight in telling people about her illness, and used it as a reason to ask her professors for deadline extensions while she worked to make everything perfect. She told people that she could never make it through graduate school, and before long others began to believe her. Eventually she dropped out of school even though the doctors were agreed that she could finish and that her seizures could be controlled with medication.

In the early stages of counseling all these issues came to the surface, but one theme appeared again and again: she never felt good enough. Jennie did not think she was good enough to be a success or to reach her goals. Whenever she would get close to succeeding, she would do something to undercut her own efforts. She would quit a job, drop out of school, lose interest in her career activities, or find other ways to defeat herself. When she came for counseling she was in her early thirties, a failure in her own eyes, and severely depressed.

## Discussion Questions

1. What is the evidence that Jennie might have had a "treatment-resistant depression" when she came for counseling?

2. Think about Jennie's life. What appear to be the major causes of her depression? What is the role of her family and her seizure disorder in causing or worsening the depression?

3. What would be your approach in counseling Jennie? What would be your counseling goals? Give reasons for your answers.

4. It has been said that anger and loss are at the foundation of most depression. Is this true of Jennie? How might this impact your counseling with her?

5. Jennie appears to repeat the same self-sabotaging cycle over and over again. Describe the cycle. How is it creating her depression? How would you help her to break free of that cycle?

6. Do you see any evidence that Jennie may be suicidal? If so, what is the evidence? How would you intervene if it appeared that Jennie might try to take her own life?

## General Questions

1. The Bible mentions depression in several places. What do the Scriptures say about depression, and how would these biblical statements apply to Jennie's case?

2. Jennie is not a Christian. She agrees with her family that religion, including Christianity, is irrelevant to contemporary life. With her attitude and her depression, how could you do Christian counseling with Jennie without alienating her and creating a deeper depression?

3. Assume that Jennie comes out of her depression. How can you help her to avoid getting depressed again in the future?

## Personal Reflection Questions

1. Reread the statement with which we began this chapter. What makes you get depressed? How do you deal with your depression?

2.  What is the evidence that you might be depressed even as you read these words? Take a few minutes to consider your answer. If you are depressed, what can you do about it? Who can help? What are the reasons that you are not getting help? When will you tell somebody about your depression? Who will you tell? Why?

3.  Assuming that you are prone to depression, how will this influence the ways in which you counsel? Be specific in your answer.

For a follow-up to the story of Jennie, please go to the Epilogue at the end of the book.

# 9

# Anxiety

"Approximately 29% of the U.S. population is estimated to have or to have had one or more diagnosable anxiety disorders at some point in their lives, making anxiety disorders the most common category of diagnoses in the ... *Diagnostic and Statistical Manual of Mental Disorders.*"* This statement from a professional journal may not apply to the community where you live or to the day on which you read these words, but one conclusion is clear: anxiety is a very common condition—one of the most common disorders that you will see as a counselor. Zoe's anxiety is an example.

Zoe was a thin, pale, twenty-year-old single college student when she came to the counselor's office. She had been referred by an academic advisor, but her difficulty was not in grades. She was a straight-A student. Instead, her problem was that she didn't have enough time to cover all the material from her classes to the level she felt was necessary. She experienced nearly constant anxiety about this and pushed herself hard, even neglecting to care for herself in the process. She reported being tired all the time, experiencing tension headaches, and having difficulty going to sleep. As she continued to talk with her counselor, Zoe shared other struggles from her life.

Socially, Zoe was very isolated. One reason, of course, was that she

* Susan Mineka and Richard Zinbarg, "A Contemporary Learning Theory Perspective on the Etiology of Anxiety Disorders," *American Psychologist* 61 (January 2006), 10.

studied all the time. In addition, she had strong judgmental attitudes that caused her to pull back from many people. She had a boyfriend who was of another race and insisted that their relationship be kept secret from everyone to avoid conflict with his parents. Zoe reported that he was verbally abusive to her, but since she was so cut off socially, she put up with it. (A few weeks into treatment, he dumped her.)

Zoe had one relative in the area—a sister with whom there was continual conflict. Zoe had the only car between the two of them, and their father, who paid for the car and their living expenses, often commanded Zoe to taxi her sister around. This bit into Zoe's study time and caused her great distress. Her sister also did many things that created conflict. For example, the sister was unorganized in her outings (such as getting groceries or going to the laundromat) and "slovenly" in her housekeeping, both of which were habits that Zoe despised and which she criticized regularly.

The parents were divorced, and Zoe did not appear to have a healthy relationship with either her mother or her father. She had a "surface" relationship with her mother, whom she saw as weak; a close relationship with her logical father, whom she perceived to be nearly infallible; and a very contentious relationship with her father's new wife. During Zoe's early years, her father was a detective and would often bring case files home. He allowed Zoe to see crime scene photos regularly, believing that she needed to know reality. For the same reason, whenever he left for work he refused to reassure Zoe that he would be back safely.

In spite of all these troubles, she reported that her most pressing concern was that she feared going to sleep lest she would die and go to hell. Zoe was a professed atheist who reported that she wanted very badly to believe in God but that the evidence just wasn't there logically. She had done a good deal of research on issues like creation versus evolution and evidence for the life and death of Christ, but her research left her unconvinced. These caused her great anguish, including more anxiety.

## Discussion Questions

1. Assume that you are Zoe's counselor. Where would you begin in your work with her? What might be your goals in counseling with her? Give reasons for your answers.

2.  Review the section on the causes of anxiety in the *Christian Counseling* book. What are the main causes of anxiety in Zoe's life? How would you deal with these?

3.  What would be ways to improve Zoe's interpersonal relationships, including relationships with members of her family?

4.  How might you be able to help with the counselee's fears about going to sleep, her fears of hell, or her "great anguish" at not being able to find convincing answers?

5.  What are the reasons for or against recommending that Zoe take medication that will reduce her anxiety? Having considered the alternatives for or against medication, which would you recommend and why?

## General Questions

1.  Summarize what the Bible says about anxiety. How might this be applied to Zoe, who is a professed atheist? How might these same principles be applied if Zoe were a Christian?

2.  In working with Zoe, would you involve other people in the counseling, such as her sister or father? Why or why not?

3.  What would you do to prepare Zoe or others like her to prevent the return of anxiety in the future? For example, next time Zoe has a test, how can she keep her anxiety under control? Be as specific as possible.

4.  What are the ethical implications of a Christian counselor talking about religious issues with Zoe? In what ways might your answer differ if the counselor was working in a Christian counseling center versus working in a secular counseling center?

## Personal Reflection Questions

1.  What creates anxiety in your life? How does it influence you? How does it interfere with smooth functioning in your life? Take time to write answers to these questions and then discuss them with a trusted friend or counselor.

2.  In what practical ways can your anxiety be reduced or better controlled because of your faith in Christ? (If you are not a Christian, ask yourself how your alternative belief system influences your anxiety.) If your Christian faith is not helping

you deal with anxiety, ask yourself why. Then discuss this privately with another person.

3.  In what types of counseling situations do you tend to get anxious? For example, some counselors get anxious when they are dealing with counselees who are in conflict, want to talk about sex, or express a lot of anger. How can you deal with these anxieties in yourself so that you are better able to help your counselees?

For a follow-up to the story of Zoe, please go to the Epilogue at the end of the book.

# 10

# Anger

Anger is an almost universal emotion, one of the first to appear and one that can cause great damage when it is out of control. Early in life we learn how to express anger, and most of us learn how to control it. Mr. J, whose story appears below, had a major problem with anger because he had not learned how to handle his anger in ways that were appropriate. His case describes an immigrant who moved to North America from a different part of the world. Even so, the principles apply wherever we live and work as counselors.

Mr. J is a thirty-five-year-old man who came to Canada four years ago with his wife, Salma, and their two children. He grew up in a large family where parental discipline was lax and where the children most often settled their differences with loud arguments and sometimes with swinging fists. This is neither unusual nor disapproved in Mr. J's country of origin. In his native culture emotions in general and anger in particular are expressed with more passion and with less restraint than is true in the suburban community where this family has settled.

Trained and experienced as a computer programmer, Mr. J was able to find work without difficulty, but he encountered problems on the job almost from the beginning. Whenever he was frustrated or disagreed with his employer or a coworker, Mr. J would explode in anger, shouting loudly, swearing, and occasionally moving toward a fight. Recently he was fired from his job after having a heated argument with his supervisor. This was the second time that he had been released from a job. In his earlier position he did not like his boss and did not comply with the company's rules. His problems then escalated when he was caught complaining about the company and his supervisors behind their backs.

Since moving into his new community, Mr. J had come to be known as a difficult and hot-tempered person who would easily get angry and violent even for trivial reasons. In a recent incident he had an argument with his neighbor, and in an outburst of rage, he broke the neighbor's window. When the neighbors called the police, Mr. J was forced to pay for the damaged property and was ordered by the court to get counseling for his out-of-control anger.

The counselor soon learned that Mr. J's anger affected his family on several levels. His wife, Salma, believed that neighbors had stopped visiting her family because of Mr. J's negativity and overreactions to insignificant irritants. The last time the family had visitors, for example, Mr. J suddenly became silent and refused to talk. Salma knew that he was angry because she could see that he was clenching his jaw and giving glaring looks of disapproval at their visitors. When the visitors left the house, Mr. J was quick to make harsh judgmental statements about them. He stated that these are bad people and insisted that his wife stop talking to them. It is not surprising that Salma feels isolated, lonely, and cut off from neighbors and others who are outside of the home. She confided to the counselor that she also feels anger toward her husband, but she keeps her feelings hidden. The children are embarrassed by their father, afraid of his anger, and most happy and relaxed when he is not present. All of this has made it harder for the family to adjust to their new homeland. When they most need support and friendship from other people, Mr. J's anger has been driving them away.

## Discussion Questions

1. What do you expect when Mr. J walks into your office for counseling? Will he be angry at you, uncooperative, repentant, excited to learn how North Americans do counseling, or inclined to express some other emotion? Give reasons for your expectations. What can you do at the beginning of the first ses-

sion to deal with any negative feelings he might have and to facilitate counseling effectiveness?

2. Mr. J and his wife are from the same country of origin. They grew up in the same community. How do you account for the fact that they respond to anger in different ways?

3. Based on your knowledge of the causes of anger, what might be causing Mr. J to be so angry? What is the evidence that his angry outbursts may reflect more than inappropriate anger expression or annoyance with his former employers and with the neighbors? How would you discover if there are other causes for his anger, including stress over trying to adjust to his new culture?

4. In what ways would you help Mr. J deal with his anger in ways that are more appropriate in his new culture and less self-destructive? How would you teach him anger-management skills?

5. Give reasons why Mr. J should have a male counselor. Give reasons why his counselor should be female. Does the counselor's gender really make a difference in this case?

6. Mr. J was referred to you for counseling. Would you seek to counsel Salma as well? Give reasons for your answer. How would you get Salma involved without arousing another outburst from her husband? Discuss reasons why the children should or should not get counseling.


## General Questions

1. Mr. J is not a Christian. With this knowledge, in what ways can you still apply biblical principles to your counseling with him?

2. In what ways would your counseling be different and more overtly Christian if Mr. J were a Christian?

3. How would you help Mr. J avoid angry outbursts in the future?

4. What follows is a quotation from the *Christian Counseling* book: When "a group of . . . counselors . . . were asked to describe their own feelings of anger . . . one counselor replied, 'We get angry when counselees are resistant to counseling despite our best efforts or when people impose upon us by making demands on our time and calling our homes when that isn't necessary.'

Most felt anger when they were attacked verbally or physically, and some said they got angry when people tried to manipulate them by demanding special attention or trying to make them feel guilty." What counselee behavior arouses anger in you? Discuss this in your group. How can you prevent these angry feelings from negatively impacting your counseling?

## Personal Reflection Questions

1. What is most likely to make you angry? Which of these causes of anger can affect your work as a counselor? What can you do to reduce the negative impact that your anger might have on others?

2. When you get angry what is your typical response? Do you shout, condemn the person who made you angry, swear, squelch your anger and pretend it does not exist, withdraw, or respond in some other way? How might any of these reactions influence your counseling? How can you prevent these reactions from impacting your counseling?

3. What are the anger styles in your life? How do these impact your interactions with others when you are angry? Which of these behaviors would you like to change? How will you do this? Be specific.

For a follow-up to the story of Mr. J, please go to the Epilogue at the end of the book.

# Guilt and Forgiveness

Forgiveness has been called the single most important concept in Christianity. Jesus came to earth to make forgiveness possible to all who want it. Within the mental health professions, however, forgiveness was largely ignored until only a few years ago. Now forgiveness has become a popular research topic in psychology. Even non-Christian counselors realize the importance of helping people deal with guilt, find forgiveness, learn to forgive others, and forgive themselves. This chapter tells the story of a Christian man who knew about divine forgiveness but who struggled with guilt and had difficulty experiencing forgiveness for himself.

Raphael works for a parachurch organization that often requires him to take business trips, sometimes to countries overseas. On one of these trips he was surprised to see a former classmate who had become a counselor and was attending a conference at the same hotel where Raphael was staying. Both men enjoyed connecting again and agreed that they would get together next time Raphael was in the area.

It happened about two months later when they went for a leisurely dinner during which Raphael mentioned almost in passing that he had a problem that nobody knew about, not even his wife. "I didn't say anything at first," the counselor said as he described Raphael's story. "I let the silence do its work, but I could feel the tension increasing. Raphael asked if we could go to a place where we could talk in private, so we got into my car and went to a park where Raphael told his story."

He started by saying that he'd been Christian all his life. His whole family went to church regularly, and for a while Raphael had a ministry with the youth at church. But in spite of his Christian commitment he had a problem that he couldn't handle. He'd been masturbating on a regular basis since he was twelve or thirteen. The counselor said that this was a problem for many men, but added that it may be better to understand persistent masturbation as a symptom of a deeper issue. At that point, Raphael started to cry. He said that for a long time he had been living two lives. One was the respected family man who did all the things that Christians are supposed to do and even worked for a Christian organization. He was faithful to his church and served the Lord there. He had been married for eight years and really loved his wife and children. But there also was a dark side to his life that nobody knew until he confessed this to his counselor friend as they sat together in the park. Raphael couldn't control his homosexual drives, so twice a month or more he went to a house where men got together just to have sex. The men there did not know each other. Nobody told their names, and they rarely had sex with the same person more than once. As he shared his story, Raphael kept crying, asking why God had created him that way.

Raphael believed that there were two parts of his emotional makeup and both needed to be fulfilled. His wife fulfilled one part, but sex with anonymous men fulfilled the other. The gay men with whom he had talked told him that the need for sex with other males was going to be there for good, and this left Raphael feeling helpless with no hope of seeing any change. He had bought into the argument that his sexual behavior was a part of him and that nothing could be changed. At times the guilt was overwhelming. He knew he was being unfaithful to his wife. He risked getting caught and losing his job, his reputation, and maybe his family. He worried lest he pick up a sexually transmitted disease and pass it on to his wife. He described how he had asked God to forgive him again and again, but every time that the temptation came back Raphael would give in and go back for more sex.

Without condoning Raphael's behavior or trying to refute his beliefs, the counselor listened to his friend, assured him that their friendship was still solid, and promised to meet next time they were in the same city. When Raphael returned on another business trip, they met again. "I had been doing a lot of thinking, praying, and research about what he was going through," the counselor said. "I couldn't find any books on bisexual married Christian men, so we just talked. Raphael told me about his childhood, his feelings for his wife, his spiritual life. Apparently he had had a good childhood, a stable family, no problems at school, and no unusual sexual experiences such as abuse." The two men discussed the issues concerning whether a person can be born with a homosexual or bisexual drive or with other sexual deviations. They agreed that regardless of one's innate tendencies some behaviors are wrong even if we feel they are right.

Raphael was defining himself by his sexual behavior. "I am homosexual" or "I am bisexual" became more important to him than "I am a child of God, loved by God, forgiven by God, and available to be cleansed and used by God." The counselor helped Raphael see that any sexual behavior outside of God's plan for sexuality eventually becomes an addiction. Raphael had become addicted to the gay sex. Like all addicts he justified his behavior with self-talk that sounded rational until he experienced an orgasm and then felt the guilt flood over his whole being. Together the men talked about how the addiction could be broken. For Raphael, the first steps had been taken. He had asked for God's forgiveness—no doubt he would have to do this again. Raphael had talked with his counselor friend, felt his acceptance, and agreed to be accountable to his friend even though they lived some distance from each other. The hardest part of their conversation concerned Raphael's wife. Should he tell her? Should he ask for her forgiveness? What if she refused to forgive? What would be the alternative if he never told his wife? Would he need her help if he was to get free of the visits to the gay sex community? Could he put aside the dark side of his personality if he never told her about it?

## Discussion Questions

1. Let us begin with the last questions. Do you think Raphael needs to tell his wife about his sex with men? Give reasons for your answer.
2. Assuming he agrees to tell his wife, how would you help him

do this? In what ways, if any, would you help him anticipate how he might respond if her reactions are angry or condemning?

3. What are the causes of Raphael's guilt? How can your knowledge of the causes help you to counsel him?

4. What are some ways by which you can help Raphael forgive himself?

5. Raphael's wife went to see a counselor after she learned about the dark side of her husband's life. Assume that she comes to you as her counselor. What would you do to help her? What goals might you have?

6. What might be the benefits of Raphael and his wife having some counseling sessions together? Why might that not be necessary? Having considered the reasons, would you recommend the joint sessions? Why?

## General Questions

1. In what specific ways was guilt adversely influencing Raphael's life?

2. Summarize biblical teaching about guilt and forgiveness that could be applied to Raphael and also to his wife.

3. As we have seen, guilt can be divided into four types. What are these types? Which apply to Raphael? In what ways, if any, would this knowledge help the counselor better understand Raphael and enable him to find forgiveness?

4. The counselor believed that Raphael had chosen to define himself by his sexuality: "I am homosexual" or "I am bisexual." Do you agree that many of us do something similar? For example, "I am incompetent." "I am a bad Christian." "I am hot tempered." How do these self-labels influence our behavior? How can they be changed to healthier thinking?

## Personal Reflection Questions

1. Take some time to think about your own life. Try to find a quiet place to do this. What secrets do you have that nobody knows about? You may want to write them down on a paper

that nobody else will find. How do these influence your life?
Look at James 5:16. Should you tell somebody about these
secrets? Why or why not? Who would you tell?

2. Throughout this book we read often about the importance of
   having others to whom we can be accountable. Think about
   your circle of friends. To whom are you accountable? If you do
   not have such a person, how can you find such a person?
   What are the advantages and disadvantages of having such a
   person?

For a follow-up to the story of Raphael, please go to the Epilogue at
the end of the book.

# 12

# Loneliness

Loneliness can take a variety of forms. It may be common in elderly people or anyone else who lives alone, but its influence goes much further. Loneliness exists in students or military personnel away from home, truck drivers and business people on extended trips, and new-comers to a community where they may be surrounded by thousands of people but don't know anyone. Loneliness also extends to children like a seven-year-old boy who was abandoned by his mother years ago and who has struggled with loneliness throughout his life. Here is the story told in his own words.

"I had a perfect life until I was seven. We had a good family. My older sister and I got along pretty well. We went to church every week, and I knew all the leaders there. But it all changed on December 16, just a few days before Christmas.

"When we came home from school that day my mother wasn't there. Some of her clothes were gone, and it looked like she had left on a trip. My dad called the police, but they couldn't find her. We didn't know whether she had just left us or if she had been kidnapped or the victim of foul play. I remember the three of us sitting in the living room on Christmas Eve. We didn't put up a tree that year, but my dad brought home some flowers. There was an article about us in the newspaper on that day before Christmas, and when the telephone rang, it was a little boy whose parents had read our story. He wanted to call to wish us a Merry Christmas.

"After the holidays we struggled for months wondering where my mother was or if she was dead. There were no answers. My dad tried to find someone to take care of us while he was at work, but his choices were not good. The first babysitter was a prostitute who watched us kids as her day job. Next we went to live with my grandmother and my uncle, but while we were there the uncle committed suicide and so we moved away. Then a missionary couple came to live with us, but one night they died in a car crash. After that my father remarried, but my sister and I did not like his new wife. We all had the attitude that 'This is tough, but the three of us will make it together.' Then the stepmother appeared, and to make things worse, she was abusive.

"Things were better at school. I found out that I was really was good at baseball. I won some trophies, and the coach wanted to help me prepare for the big leagues. He gave me a lot of time, attention, coaching, and encouragement, but in the middle of this my family moved and I lost contact with this man who really cared for me. Then one night when I was about twelve, my mother called from Canada. We found out that she had gone away to live with another man, had three children with him, but now was divorced. She went to court to get visitation rights to see my sister and me, but we didn't want to see her because she had abandoned us and caused so much pain, depression, and loneliness in our lives.

"I am now fifty-three years old. I have had one problem after another since my mother left on that Christmas so many years ago. I have had drug problems and a drinking problem. I was married for fourteen years, but the marriage ended in divorce. We had two sons that I love a lot. One visits me sometimes and brings his little girl (my granddaughter) to see me, but I don't know where the other son is. Some time ago my closest buddy died because of a motorcycle accident. I don't have a very good job, I don't have many work skills, and I live by myself in a small apartment that is depressing for me.

"When I was a teenager I dropped out of church, but about two years ago I came back. To be honest I visited several churches but did not feel welcome at any of them. I guess they didn't think I fit. Then I found my present church. The pastor meets with me every week and has been very helpful, although there are times when we don't agree. About six months ago I volunteered to clean the church on Saturdays before the weekend services. It helps get me out of that dingy little apartment.

"Every year the worst times for me are around Christmas. All of the old memories come back about my mother going away. Usually I have no place to go, so often I drink to hide the pain. When I started cleaning the church they gave me a key to the building, so last Christmas night I went to the church. There was nobody there. I walked down the aisle and up on to the platform. Then I looked around at the darkened building and the empty seats. I thought, 'What am I doing here? Has my life come to this?' I felt very much alone. I still do."

## Discussion Questions

1. Review the main causes of loneliness. Which of these appear in the life of this man? Does attachment theory help account for his loneliness? How could your knowledge about the causes of loneliness influence your counseling?
2. What is the role of Christmas in this man's case? Notice that he remembers the date his mother left and the day of the newspaper article. How could you deal with the impact of Christmas in helping the counselee get free of his loneliness?
3. What would be your goals in counseling with this man? In addition to his loneliness, what other problem areas would you address? Why?
4. Would you try teaching social, vocational, money management, or other skills to this man? What skills does he need? How could he get them? Be as practical as possible.
5. Assume that some well-intentioned friend comes to this counselee and says, "If you're lonely, just get out and find some friends. You are not apartment bound or sick in bed. So quit feeling sorry for yourself and get out to meet others. There are lots of people in your church. Just get to know them." Evaluate this advice. How could it be helpful to the counselee? Why might it be harmful?

## General Questions

1. Assume that this counselee decides to get close to Jesus, who "sticks closer than a brother." Will this spiritual activity help

with the loneliness? Why would it help? Why might it be of little or no help?

2.  What is the role of the bar where this person drinks every year on Christmas Eve and occasionally at other times when he is lonely? What are the alternatives to the bar? As a counselor, how could you stimulate people in the church to help this man resist the annual Christmas temptation to deal with his loneliness by drinking?

3.  Look up *abandonment* on the Internet and read some of the postings. How can this help you counsel better with this counselee? How do you think the counselee would be helped if he did a similar Internet search?

## Personal Reflection Questions

1.  What was the loneliest time in your life? Think of something specific. What caused the loneliness? In what ways can these reflections on your own loneliness help you to be a better counselor with lonely people?

2.  How lonely are you at present? What makes you lonely? Realistically, what can you do about it? Who will hold you accountable to take some actions to deal with your loneliness? Be specific.

3.  What feelings or biases do you have toward people who are lonely? Do you tend to withdraw from them, criticize them, ignore them, or smother them with attention? How do your attitudes differ, for example, when the lonely person also is homeless, elderly, from another country, divorced, gay, in the military, or non-Christian? What are the reasons for your attitudes and actions?

4.  How might Jesus respond to your attitudes and actions toward lonely people? How could your attitudes impact the ways in which you counsel with lonely people? How can you change? What are reasons that you should change? What are reasons that you should stay the same as you are?

For a follow-up to this story, please go to the Epilogue at the end of the book.

## PART THREE

# Developmental Issues

# 13

# Childhood

"A review of the counseling literature reveals numerous attempts to fit children into an adult counseling framework, with suggestions to engage children by asking questions and other verbally based means." This is the observation of Garry Landreth, a counselor who specializes in working with young people. He notes that adult methods often fail to work with children because they differ from adults "psychologically and cognitively, and their ability to communicate is uniquely different from that of adults. Developmentally, children do not think in abstract forms," and they lack the verbal competencies to express what they feel. Because of this, counseling with children requires a shift from simply adapting basic adult-counseling skills to approaches that use new and child-appropriate methods. Please keep this in mind as you ponder the story of five-year-old Vanessa.

When she was brought to see a counselor, Vanessa was only five years old. Her parents were in the process of getting a divorce, and the young counselee lived in the midst of ongoing parental conflict, disagreement, shouting, and name calling. As the relationship between her parents had become more unfriendly and acrimonious, Vanessa had begun acting out in school. She was disobedient, irritable, impatient, and increasingly inclined to hit or to argue with the other kids. She also cried easily and told both her teacher and her counselor that nobody loved her, that nobody cared about her, and that she wanted to die. Based on her experience in working with children, the counselor concluded that all these behaviors and comments were Vanessa's ways of expressing her emotions and insecurities as her family appeared to be disintegrating and she was feeling abandoned and alone.

The counselor wanted to help Vanessa express what she was feeling inside and get assurance that she would be secure and not be abandoned. Vanessa liked to draw, so she was given crayons and asked to draw pictures of her family. The placement of the figures and their activities in the drawings revealed some of the family interactions that Vanessa might not have been able to describe in words. At one point the counselor and Vanessa talked about simple feelings such as being happy, sad, excited, or scared. Then they picked a color to go with each feeling. For Vanessa, happy was green, sad was black, scared was "yellow like pee" because Vanessa explained that when she got scared sometimes she wet her pants. At times the counselor would draw a stick figure of Vanessa or of a family member and ask the girl to color how that person was feeling. Along the way Vanessa learned that it was OK to have several colors (feelings) at the same time.

The counseling sessions always had an open play time. Vanessa could choose from a great variety of dolls, puppets, fake foods, jewelry, games, cars or trucks, and other items that often became the catalyst for stories that Vanessa made up or for comments she made in passing. Often these informal statements were revealing about her family or herself but without requiring Vanessa to sit in a chair like an adult and talk about her insecurities or emotions. Sometimes the counselor and counselee would "make up new stories" that would be designed to reassure Vanessa and enable her to see that there could be stability and love from her parents even if they got a divorce and one of them moved away.

### Discussion Questions

1.  Unlike many adults, children have very little power or control over their environments or over the actions of parents and other adults. Assume that the parents are getting marriage counseling but as Vanessa's counselor you would like to talk to her mother and father about the child living in the midst of their crumbling marriage. What would be your goals in talking to the parents? How could this be of help to Vanessa?

2. The parents may disagree on many things, but suppose they both want what is best for their daughter. They ask for your guidance in what they can do to parent effectively during this stressful time in their lives. What would you recommend?

3. Summarize the causes of Vanessa's insecurities.

4. What would be the goals of your counseling with her?

5. In addition to the use of play and drawings, what other methods would you use in your work with Vanessa?

## General Questions

1. Assume that you are working in a Christian counseling center. As a Christian counselor, in what specific ways will your commitment to Christ influence your counseling with Vanessa?

2. Answer the previous question again but with the assumption that you are working in a government-sponsored counseling facility where any references to God or to religion are discouraged or not permitted.

3. In counseling with children like Vanessa, are there other consultants or adults, apart from the parents, that you would want to involve with your work? For example, how could Vanessa's kindergarten teacher be a partner in helping you to understand and help this little girl?

4. List specific actions that could be taken to prevent further problems in Vanessa's life as her parents separate.

## Personal Reflection Questions

1. Imagine that as a counselor or counseling student you are assigned to work directly with children, doing work similar to what Vanessa's counselor has done. What would be your feelings about this assignment? What insecurities would you have, if any? What is the evidence that you would be effective or ineffective in working directly with children?

2. Assuming that you would like to work with children, what additional training would you need that you do not have now? How would you get this training?

3. Over the years significant evidence has accumulated to support

the conclusion that parental conflict and divorce can have a negative influence on children, even when the children are grown and their parents separate. In what ways has the relationship between your parents impacted you? Be specific. Consider writing your answers in a journal and perhaps sharing them with a friend.

4. In what ways have early conflicts or insecurities in your home, abuse, or other early experiences influenced you even today? In what ways will these background experiences influence your counseling? What can be done to help you overcome these past influences so that they do not adversely affect your life and your counseling? Be specific in your answers.

For a follow-up to the story of Vanessa, please go to the Epilogue at the end of the book.

# 14

# Adolescence

Adolescence has been described as a time of "storm and stress." The pressures, options, and complexities in our open and pluralistic culture have raised the intensity of the storm and increased the level of stress. All of this can be seen in the case of Mark, whose story is told in the words of his counselor.

"When the Gothic teenager walked into my office for his initial visit, I had this overwhelming feeling that I was in for a wild ride. Mark's Mohawk* almost touched the top of the doorframe as he swaggered across the room and sank as deep into his chair as humanly possible. He obviously was not bothered by the 'emergency' that had led his school principal to order this counseling session. Mark had threatened to blow up the school. Understandably, this had shaken the school administrators. In contrast, Mark did not seem to be at all surprised at the commotion. In fact he appeared to be happy to be stirring the pot with those in authority over him.

---

* For readers who might not be familiar with this term, a Mohawk is a hairstyle, popular with teenagers in some parts of the world. Most often the head is shaved except for one wide strip of hair going from the front of the forehead to the back of the neck and treated to stand straight up. Sometimes the hair is brightly colored. Photos of a Mohawk hairstyle are available on the Internet. The phrase "Gothic teenager" refers to a young person who often dresses completely in black, sometimes including black eyeliner and black fingernail polish.

"As I started the session with Mark, I was more than prepared to spend the next fifty minutes with an individual that I wouldn't like very much. Yeah, I admit, Mohawks sometimes have that effect on me. But a funny thing happened about fifteen or twenty minutes into the session. I realized that I liked Mark. He was funny, quick, intelligent, and even caring. For a fourteen-year-old with a Mohawk, Mark was a real good kid. I was actually very surprised that he had threatened to hurt so many people, so I asked about his intention to blow up the school. He answered bluntly, 'I was never going to do it. My English teacher wanted a passionate paper. I figure blowing up a bunch of Catholic school kids is pretty exciting reading.' Mark reported that he was never serious about bombing the cafeteria, but he was serious about garnering the attention of his classmates and teachers. In fact, Mark thrived on breaking the rules at the church school, and he looked for any opportunity to make a stir.

"In regard to my job for this first session, the school had requested an evaluation to determine Mark's risk of harm to others. Basically, they wanted my assurance that Mark would not blow up the school.

"Mark had had a very difficult family life. His mother was very involved in his daily activities, and it is probably fair to describe her posture with Mark as overprotective. Mark had two siblings. His older sister was an insurance executive who made a substantial income. His older brother was an accomplished mechanic. Both his brother and his sister opted to stay at home rather than move out of the family home after they finished their college degrees. And both were merciless in their interaction with Mark. They tried to control his behavior, often made fun of him, and sometimes tried to punish him for breaking the family rules. Although Mark's relationship with his mother and siblings was difficult, his relationship with his father was perhaps the most problematic. Basically, Mark's dad ignored him. Although the two older siblings enjoyed positive relationships with their dad, Mark was unable to connect with him on even the most basic level. When Mark's dad did speak to him, it was usually to correct him or to ask him to do some chore around the house."

After the initial counseling session, the school requested that the counselor continue to meet with Mark.

## Discussion Questions

1. As a counselor, would you be willing to assure the principal that Mark would not blow up the school? On what basis would you make your assessment?
2. Assume that Mark is coming to you for an appointment after the initial assessment that the counselor described. How would you start this second session? What would be your goals for counseling?
3. Which of the teenage personalities might Mark fit, as defined by the Barna Research Group?
4. Could you give an explanation for Mark's apparent delight in "breaking the rules at the church school" and looking "for any opportunity to make a stir"?
5. What approaches would you take in counseling with Mark?
6. To what extent are Mark's problems related to his family situation?
7. What is Mark's bizarre dress about? Is it merely a teenage phase, or is it clinically significant?
8. Mark was described as "funny, quick, intelligent, and even caring." How would you draw on these characteristics to improve your counseling with Mark?

## General Questions

1. How would you counsel Mark or somebody like him if the counselee did not particularly want counseling but he or she had been referred by some person in authority or ordered by a judge to get counseling?
2. How would you handle the issue of getting Mark's trust and maintaining confidentiality if he had been ordered to get counseling by some other person who was paying for the counseling and was expecting a report of the progress?
3. In what ways could you help Mark to mature into adulthood without squelching his personality but also without him getting into further trouble?

### Personal Reflection Question

1. Be honest. What do you think about Mark and his "passionate" essay written for the English teacher? The case study written by the counselor suggests that he enjoyed meeting with Mark. Did you sense (like the author of this book sensed) that the counselor may even have enjoyed Mark's prank and the commotion that ensued? This was not funny to the school principal, but do you wonder if the counselor might have found it amusing without admitting this to anybody? Counseling is serious work, dealing with serious problems, but do you think that you ever will be amused at some activity of a counselee or that you might even secretly admire some counselee's determination to shake up another person's complacency? If this ever happens, how will you deal with these feelings of amusement or admiration? Discuss this with some other counselor or counseling students.

For a follow-up to the story of Mark, please go to the Epilogue at the end of the book.

# Twenties and Thirties

Almost every chapter in this book presents a similar dilemma: how to select one story to illustrate the complexities of a major problem area. This chapter is among those where a single case did not appear to be enough, so I have provided the story of a twenty-three-year-old woman from a traditional Christian family and a thirty-two-year-old man whose life appears to be anything but traditional. Perhaps their similarities and differences will illustrate the many uniquenesses of people in their twenties and thirties.

## CASE STORY 1—Melissa

Melissa is a twenty-three-year-old single female who has requested counseling services to address her symptoms of depression. These include fatigue, a depressed mood, weight gain, and loss of energy. She reports experiencing mild bouts with depression at multiple times in the past. Melissa is a recent college graduate, currently working in a job that will end after two years of employment. She is about halfway through that time but reports that she is not particularly interested in the work. Melissa has a boyfriend whom she "expects to marry someday" and who is very supportive and concerned about her depression.

Melissa grew up as a Christian in a "strongly fundamentalist" church and home environment. Legalism was a pervasive dynamic, and relationships were strongly hierarchical. Melissa's father made most of the decisions for the family, the mother supported this system of responsibility, and it clearly was taught by their church. Melissa was always obedient to this teaching, even to the point of following the college major her father chose for her. In her third year at college, however, she began to attend another church that was closer to school. Melissa reported feeling relieved that she didn't have to go home every weekend but could stay at school instead and build relationships there. The new church is different doctrinally from her home church and strongly emphasizes grace rather than rules. Melissa has been affected deeply by these new ideas and is very devoted to rebuilding her spiritual life around grace, moving away from legalism. Her family disapproves of these "heretical" ideas, but she has maintained this newer stance. Even so, she struggles greatly with defining who she is and understanding her uniqueness in the face of her new theological beliefs and her family's resistance.

Melissa did not really like the college major that was chosen by her father. Nevertheless, she finished her studies in that area even though she has never had a desire to work in the field she studied. She had taken her present position as a way to "tread water" while she figures out how to proceed. Her parents keep urging her to look for a job in the field that she studied. Instead, Melissa has been so struck by the new experience of grace that she wants more to please God in her vocation than to please her parents. Her only thought about how to do this has been to consider opportunities in Christian ministry. She has been moving in that direction for a year, but this is not proving to be a good fit, so Melissa is at a loss about what is the right thing to do at this point.

## CASE STORY 2—Phil

Phil is a thirty-two-year-old male with a master's degree in business and a very good job at a large software development company. He grew up in a Christian home and still has good rapport with his parents, although he seems reluctant to give many details of his background. He greatly admires his dad, who is very successful in his profession, but Phil is closer to his mother, whose counsel he takes seriously. She appears to be a strong person who has been very direct in telling her son that he needs counseling.

When he entered the counselor's office, Phil had no hesitation in stating his problems. He described himself as being continually anxious and both awkward and uncomfortable in relating to people. He stated that he was addicted to work, alcohol, and sex. Earlier in his life he had been abused sexually, but he did not go into any details except to indicate that the abuse had not occurred at home. At present he lives alone and freely admits that he does not eat well and watches too much television. Phil has a number of personality quirks that make it hard for him to connect relationally with the community that he needs so desperately.

Recently, Phil has been attending an emergent church. He gives a lot of money to the church, but the pastor wonders if this may be an attempt for Phil to make up for his feelings of being such a failure as a Christian. He wants to serve in ways that will help him find value, acceptance, and a sense of belonging, but the church leaders are reluctant to give him responsibility because of his apparent instability. He looks at everyone else in the church, many of whom are young like Phil, assumes that they are all doing really well, and fails to realize that many are equally broken. None of the church leaders feels equipped to help Phil, including the pastor who decides to send him to a counselor. "He needs a life makeover and the structure to maintain it," the pastor says in his referral. "Phil is so up and down and inconsistent that it is sad. He has no direction and no clear plan for his life."

## Discussion Questions

Melissa and Phil are of different ages, gender, and backgrounds. They live in different places and have different issues that they bring to their counselors. Together, however, their lives show some of the challenges that counselors face in working with people in this diverse and ever-changing twenty to thirty age group. You may want to consider the following questions, first by looking at the case of Melissa and then by applying these same questions to Phil.

1. Summarize the major issues that the counselee is facing. Which of these problems or challenges, if any, is typical of people in their twenties and thirties?
2. Assume that you are the counselor. What approach would you take? Why?

3. Each of these people appears to be struggling to find identity and direction. How would you help them find what they are seeking? Please be precise in your answer.

4. Does Phil really need a "life makeover and the structure to maintain it"? What about Melissa? If the answer is "yes," how would you bring about a life makeover?

5. Consider these words from the *Christian Counseling* book: "Yale researchers found that many young people have a 'Dream' of the kind of life they want to lead. This Dream is an imaginary picture of what life could be like.... Life circumstances, parents, or friends may encourage or interfere with the Dream, but regardless of what others may think, this Dream can generate excitement, vitality, and life purpose. The Yale research team demonstrated that people who build their lives around a Dream in early adulthood have a better chance for personal fulfillment, even though there may be times of struggle in maintaining the commitment and working toward the Dream's fulfillment. When there is no Dream, people drift." Do these counselees have a Dream? Describe it. If they do not have a Dream, what can you do to help them get a Dream and fulfill it? Is that your job as a counselor? Give reasons for your answer.

6. What will you do if they do not want to pursue a Dream?

7. In counseling, it is easy to use basic psychological principles and never mention Christ, use Christian principles, or reflect on biblical teaching as you counsel. Where would Christ be in your counseling with Melissa and Phil? What is there about your counseling that could be considered Christian counseling? If you cannot think of an answer, why is this?

8. What are the signs of hope for each of these counselees?

## General Questions

1. What is the role of the church in the life of each of these counselees? What could the church community be doing to supplement the work of the counselor? In what ways could the church replace the work of the counselor or the need for counseling? Be specific.

2. What is the role of parents in helping each counselee make progress forward? In what specific ways can the counselor stimulate healthy parental involvement? Should this be a goal of counseling?
3. As a counselor, what can you be doing to understand the issues that face people in their twenties and thirties?
4. As a counselor, what can you be doing to prevent some of the problems that people face in their twenties and thirties?
5. Share some stories of people who have messed up their lives when they were under age thirty-five or forty but who have been turned around and even been used by God in significant ways. What caused the turnaround?

## Personal Reflection Questions

1. As you read the chapter on twenties and thirties in *Christian Counseling*, what issues applied to you? What insecurities or personal concerns did the chapter arouse in you? How will you deal with these issues? Write your answers in a journal that can be kept in a safe place so your private reflections will not be read by others. Please try to answer these questions even if you are not in this age group.
2. If the chapter and the case studies have raised personal issues in you, with what trusted person will you discuss these issues? If you choose not to discuss these issues with anybody, give reasons for your decision.
3. What is your Dream? If you do not have one, how can you get one? Why might you decide that you do not want a Dream? If you have a Dream, how do you turn it into reality? What or who gets in the way of your progress toward fulfilling the Dream?
4. Respond to this statement: "Where there is no Dream, people drift."

For a follow-up to the stories of Melissa and Phil, please go to the Epilogue at the end of the book.

# 16

# Forties and Fifties

This is the story of a man who agreed to be interviewed for this book. The details of his life are unique, but his experiences seem typical of so many people who are like him. They are at the prime of life. It is a time when many men and women are in careers that are well established, have personal life directions that are clearly set, are watching their children move into early adulthood, and are living lives to the fullest. But Don is not there. He feels directionless, frustrated, and aware that the years are passing, along with opportunities and hope for the future. Don is fifty-three, remarried, and male, but his struggles appear with equal frequency in those who are at a different age, with a different marital status, and either male or female.

At the beginning of the interview, Don mentioned *Mr. Holland's Opus*, a 1995 movie about a man who wanted to be a composer but took a job as a high school teacher to pay the bills. The job was supposed to be a temporary position, but Mr. Holland stayed for many years, impacting hundreds of students with his life, trying to compose his musical opus on weekends and summer vacations, never realizing that his students were the real legacy of his life. Don feels a kinship with Mr. Holland. Since he was a boy, growing up in an intellectually stimulating home, Don had wanted to be a novelist, but like Mr. Holland, Don also took a temporary job that has lasted for years. On the weekends he still works on his writing but seems no closer to getting anything published.

Don grew up in a college town where his mother taught high school and his father was a professor. In view of his interests, it is not surprising that Don majored in journalism, but he felt held back by insecurities and he never had the assertiveness to make a success in his chosen field. After working at a couple of newspapers, he took a job in the editorial department of a textbook publisher and has been in the publishing business for most of his working life. When he was in his twenties, Don got married to a woman who went to his church, and eventually the couple had two children. After a few years, however, the marriage ended in divorce, and when he was forty-two Don moved to another part of the country so he could start over.

Alone in a city where he did not know anybody except other people at work, Don started visiting churches on the weekends, trying to connect especially with others who might be single and his age. In the smaller churches he felt like a misfit in the midst of the programs for couples, and the singles activities focused on unmarried people of college age. In the mega-churches, he felt lost and unwelcome. Eventually he remarried, and after four years together the couple gets along fine, but Don's wife is busy with her career and he still works at his writing. They attend church on a regular basis and sometimes have a Sunday lunch with another couple or with one or two friends, but then they go home to their apartment. There Don's wife sometimes watches TV or gets ready for the week ahead at work. He sits at his computer and works on the novel that he hopes to someday publish so that it will influence people like Mr. Holland impacted his students.

Don is not a social misfit. He is quiet and somewhat shy with a personality that is not especially vivacious or engaging, but he is a likable person who clearly is intelligent and well read. He is regarded positively at his place of work and gets along well with his coworkers, but he has never actively pursued other opportunities in his company and seems to be content where he is. At times he looks for other jobs and sometimes goes for interviews, but nothing has opened up. Occasionally he wonders what it would be like if he were a teacher or in ministry, but he does not have the training for these professions, and since he still pays alimony to his former wife, he lacks the money and motivation to get more education. He likes attending seminars and retreats, but usually he goes by himself because his wife has other interests and he has not built many friendships.

Don feels that he is drifting through life. His life is stable but uneventful. His career is worthwhile but not especially fulfilling. His spiritual life is consistent but does not appear to be growing. His relationships with people are cordial, but he does not feel close to anybody.

## Discussion Questions

1. Assume that Don comes to you for counseling. He does not bring a major problem like depression or anxiety, but he would like help in getting some life direction so that he does not feel like he is drifting through life. How would you help him?

2. What would be the hardest obstacles for you to overcome in your work with Don or people like him?

3. What psychological changes may be impacting Don at this time in his life? What physiological changes may be taking place? In what ways does your knowledge of these changes impact how you would counsel Don?

4. Are there skills that Don needs to learn (such as communication skills or relationship skills)? What are these skills? What is the evidence that Don does not have the skills that you suggest? How could you help him get these needed skills? Be specific.

5. Would you encourage Don to find a new job or a different position in his company? Give reasons for your answer.

## General Questions

1. Don is a man in his fifties who appears to be drifting through life. Who do you know who is like Don? Describe this person and explain why he or she is drifting.

2. Assume that this person is your friend. Are there ways that you can help or encourage your friend apart from counseling? Be specific. Is it ethical to give this help even though your friend has not asked for it? Why or why not?

3. Who do you know in their forties or fifties who is not drifting through life but who, instead, is finding life to be fulfilling? Contrast this person you know with Don. What makes the dif-

ference? How could your answers to these questions apply to your work with counselees like Don?

4. Erik Erickson wrote that mentoring and generativity are important if one is to have fulfillment at Don's age. How can this apply to Don? Be specific.

5. The church did not help Don very much, especially when he was single. How can the church be more sensitive to the needs of single people like Don when he first arrived in his new community? To what extent would a single person of Don's age find acceptance and community in your church? What could your church be doing that is different to minister to people like Don and his wife?

## Personal Reflection Questions

1. In what ways are you like Don? Even if you are of a different age, occupation, or marital status, do you feel at times like you are drifting? Why? What can you do about this? Write your answers in a journal and discuss them with a person you trust and respect.

2. Read these words from the *Christian Counseling* book: "to avoid stagnation in the forties and fifties, we need to be involved in working to establish and guide the next generation." This mentoring is "a one-to-one reaching out to people who are younger, needy, and/or eager to learn. Teachers [like Mr. Holland] and professors have unusual opportunities to reach out in this way, but so do counselors, parents, business leaders, and any person who has contact with younger people. Mentors of any age experience the satisfaction of knowing that their lives and observations can be meaningful and useful to others." Who are you mentoring and/or who is mentoring you? Would you agree that everybody needs at least one mentor and that most of us need to be mentoring at least on other person? Give reasons for your answer.

For a follow-up to the story of Don, please go to the Epilogue at the end of the book.

# The Later Years

Older people (like those who are younger) differ significantly in their attitudes, responses to adversity, general outlook on life, and perspectives on the future. The following case describes an elderly lady who had been active and positive in her life perspective until recently. As you read her story, remember that the elderly can benefit from a counselor's services just as much as counselees who are much younger.

Rachel Jones is an eighty-nine-year-old woman who lives alone in an apartment in a retirement community. During the past several months Ms. Jones has experienced a rapid decline in her ability to walk because of rheumatoid arthritis in both of her knees. This has severely limited her social life, which formerly included chairing the library committee, attending church services with other residents, and participating in cultural excursions such as going to museums and plays. Now the extent of her social contact includes talking with in-home care-givers and weekly calls from her daughter, who lives in another state.

Ms. Jones was recently referred to behavioral health services because her care-givers noticed that she was not attending to her hygiene or paying her bills on time. In addition, Ms. Jones reported that she was having difficulty with her memory. Ms. Jones' daughter also contacted the nursing staff at her retirement community and informed them that Ms. Jones had recently been calling more frequently in the evenings, crying. After a thorough neuropsychological evaluation, Ms. Jones' cognitive abilities were found to be average to above average for her age. The clinician who prepared the report ruled out dementia, but suggested that Ms. Jones was likely suffering from memory problems related to clinical depression.

Ms. Jones has now been referred to you for counseling. The nursing staff and care-givers have made it clear to you that she is insistent upon being called "Rachel" rather than Ms. Jones. During your intake interview you learn several important pieces of information that may be relevant to treatment.

- Rachel Jones holds a doctorate in pharmacy. Although she does not make a big issue of the matter, it is clear that her title has been disregarded at some point in the process of her move to the retirement community. She appears to enjoy the recognition when you acknowledge her by her proper title.
- Dr. Jones has outlived her husband of fifty-six years (who died eight years ago), two children (who died three and twelve years ago, respectively), and most of her friends.
- Dr. Jones has no previous history of depression or other psychological disorders.
- This lady's recent physical decline has sparked end-of-life concerns that were not present when she was more socially active. She now feels like her only role in life is to be a patient and that others don't seem to expect much from her.
- Throughout her life Dr. Jones has attended church regularly, but her faith does not appear to be a significant part of her life at present.

## Discussion Questions

1. Summarize the major issues that Dr. Jones appears to be facing. Which of these problems or challenges, if any, is typical of people in their later years?
2. What do you know about development in the later years that would influence the ways in which you would approach counseling with Dr. Jones?
3. In your relationship to Dr. Jones, what dynamics may you need to monitor closely because you are counseling an older adult who is also a former health professional?

4. What approaches might you suggest to Dr. Jones' care-givers and family members to help her most effectively? Would you discuss these suggestions with Dr. Jones prior to sharing them with her care-givers? Why would you check with Dr. Jones first? Why would you not check with her first? What would you do if she does not give you permission to share your suggestions with her care-givers?

5. Please suggest other resources and activities outside of your counseling which might help Dr. Jones feel valued and connected to others in a meaningful way.

## General Questions

1. What problems might you anticipate in a person who is the age of Dr. Jones? What causes problems in old age? What is the possibility that your knowledge of these problems might lead you to look for and to find problems that really are not there?

2. The *Christian Counseling* book lists four significant issues that "new elder" older people face.
   - The question of identity: Who am I?
   - The question of community: Where do I belong?
   - The question of passion: What do I care about?
   - The question of meaning: What is my legacy?

   Would you raise any of these issues with Dr. Jones? Why would you raise these issues? What are reasons for not raising them?

3. When, if ever, would you bring spiritual issues into your counseling with Dr. Jones? How could you introduce the spiritual issues if Dr. Jones does not appear to be interested? Discuss the ethics of introducing spiritual issues if the client has not requested this. Discuss the ethical and theological implications of ignoring spiritual issues if you are a committed follower of Jesus Christ.

## Personal Reflection Questions

1. What is ageism? What is the evidence that some prejudices against the elderly exist in you? Write about this in your jour-

nal. Ask somebody who knows you well to give an honest opinion of whether and to what extent prejudice against old people might exist in you. What can you do to remove the ageism that might exist in you?

2.  What myths do you have about aging? How do you know these attitudes are myths?

3.  Look at question 2 in the *General Questions* section above. Reflect on the four questions as they apply to you, in your life, now. Write answers in your journal and consider discussing these issues with somebody you trust and respect.

4.  In what ways are your attitudes toward aging influenced by grandparents or other older people that you know or have known? If these experiences have been negative, how can you prevent these negative experiences from influencing your counseling with older counselees?

For a follow-up to the story of Dr. Rachel Jones, please go to the Epilogue at the end of the book.

## PART FOUR

# Interpersonal Issues

# 18

# Conflict and Relationships

According to the Christian Camping and Conference Association, "Camping has long been considered one of Christianity's most effective mediums for impacting lives and growing the Church. For decades, clergy and lay leaders in all denominations have realized that the spiritually focused, challenge-oriented temporary community inherent in Christian camping is unsurpassed for igniting faith, instilling character, and implanting ideals in participants, regardless of age or background. Christian camping is also considered by many to be the best means for inspiring an individual to a life of service.... Millions of people, young and old, take part in traditional and unusual programs all through the year, and hundreds of thousands make significant spiritual decisions during or following the camping experience." The story that follows involves a Christian camp where conflict developed, tensions built, and relationships were strained as the camp leaders dealt with a major disagreement.

Camp Sunrise—the name is fictitious, but everything else in this story is true—was founded almost forty years ago by a group of dedicated church leaders in a country where Christians are in the minority. For many years, waves of campers would come every summer for six days of recreation and Christian teaching, far from the busy cities and rural villages where many of them lived. As the years passed, the camp programs remained unchanged. The leaders did things as they had done from the beginning, without realizing (or admitting) that the younger generation was changing. Eventually, some of the young campers grew up and became camp leaders themselves under the direction and watchful eyes of the experienced Christians who had founded and developed the camp over the years.

As they would talk among themselves, the new generation of leaders agreed that Camp Sunrise had lost touch with the young people that they were committed to reach. In the early days there were long church services every morning and evening with lengthy sermons about theological doctrines that are important but that left the young audiences bored and itching to escape. Four decades after the camp had first opened, the same long sermons started and ended each camper's day. Nothing had changed, and finally the young leaders decided to express their frustration. They met first with the camp director, argued politely that things needed to change, and suggested practical steps to give Camp Sunrise and the campers a new approach, new vision, and new ways to reach people in an emerging digital age. The camp director, a kindly man in his sixties, agreed, but when the old guard learned of the proposed changes, they were both shocked and resistant. They urged the camp director to hold firm to the old ways. They argued that new approaches would weaken the camp theology and bring in new methods and teaching that would undercut the theological foundations on which the camp had been built. More disconcerting to them, perhaps, was the fact that the change advocates were all camp alumni and they were led by a twenty-five-year-old who was well known to everybody. The proponents of change were not angry young men and women; they had carefully considered new approaches to camping and even had a plan for making the programs more relevant without undercutting the biblical basis of the camping experience.

As opening day approached, the division got wider. The old guard felt threatened, undermined, unappreciated, and angry. They argued that these twenty- and thirty-year-olds were too young to give leadership, not evangelistic enough, too liberal, too interested in creative programs that would teach the campers in ways other than the theologically solid sermons that had been given for so many years. The advocates for change felt that they were not being heard or respected. They knew that the campers were becoming increasingly frustrated and consistently bored. The issues that concerned them—issues like relationships, dating, or career choice—were never addressed in the long sermons about the Trinity or church doctrine, sermons that now were given by older men who had lost touch with the young audiences that they were trying to influence.

Everybody got together two days before the first campers were scheduled to arrive. The camp director chaired the meeting, but he appeared pressured and overwhelmed by the conflict, wanting to please both sides, but knowing that each group was expecting him to rule in their favor. For more than an hour representatives from each side presented their arguments and counter-arguments. To their credit, both sides tried to remain calm and not combative, but feelings were running high because the future direction of the camp appeared to be on the line. Somebody in the room stated that the camp needed to have unity in the staff. He suggested that God was unlikely to give his blessing to an organization that was so deeply divided. Before they ended the meeting, the people present would need to make a decision and then move forward with as much unity as possible.

## Discussion Questions

1. For purposes of discussion, let us assume that the chairman called for a break at this point. You are a counselor-observer who is present at the meeting. The chairman asks your opinion about what should be done next. What would you tell him?
2. Assume further that the chairman asks you to meet briefly with both sides and then chair the meeting. How would you proceed?
3. This is a Christian group. What biblical principles would you bring to the group when they reconvene?
4. Reread the section titled "The Causes of Conflict and Problems in Interpersonal Relations" in the *Christian Counseling* book. Summarize the causes of the conflict in the Camp Sunrise story. How would your awareness of these causes be applied to your counseling with group?
5. Now look at the section in the *Christian Counseling* book titled "Counseling, Conflicts and Interpersonal Relations." Which of these principles would you apply to this group? Why would you choose these?

6. If the leaders of the two sides had an angry and adversarial relationship, what would you do if you were to meet with them in an effort to calm the situation and help them resolve their differences?

## General Questions

1. The director of Camp Sunrise was chairing the meeting, but he is described as appearing "pressured and overwhelmed by the conflict, wanting to please both sides, but knowing that each group was expecting him to rule in their favor." Specifically, what could you do to help him in this situation that was so difficult for him?

2. Think of a conflict situation with which you are familiar. It could be conflict in a family, workplace, church, committee, parachurch organization, or college, or a conflict between two people who have been friends for a long time. Please get a specific situation in mind. How could you apply your knowledge of counseling and conflict resolution to this situation? If you are meeting in a group, decide on one or two of the situations with which you are familiar and apply your answers there.

3. Erik Barnett was a missionary leader who helped shape the African Inland Mission. When he was asked how he handled discord among missionaries, he gave a simple formula. First he met with each side to listen. Then if he sensed continued tension he would gather all the missionaries together and say "Now there are two things that I'm going to ask you. (1) Do you have a *daily* prayer meeting together, and (2) do you have a *monthly* business meeting together to talk out the work that you're doing?" Mr. Barnett added that "invariably they would have let those two things drop. When we got those things re-established harmony came back again." What do you think of this formula? What are your reasons for agreeing or disagreeing? Give reasons why this would have worked or not worked in the case of Camp Sunrise.

**Personal Reflection Questions**

1. What conflicts are in your life at present? How are these conflicts affecting you? Please be specific. Consider writing your answers to these questions in a journal. Could a counselor or trusted friend help you deal with the conflict in your life? Who would that person be and why would you ask for help? When will you ask for help?

2. In his book *The Coward's Guide to Conflict,* Dr. Tim Ursiny notes that most of us dislike conflict and prefer to avoid it. How do you respond to conflict that involves you personally? How do you respond in the presence of conflict that might involve others or that might be within a group of which you are a part? What are the reasons for your reactions? What can you do that will enable you to be less threatened and uncomfortable in the presence of conflict?

3. How will your personal responses to conflict impact what you do as a counselor whenever there are people engaged in conflict in your office?

For a follow-up to the story of Camp Sunrise, please go to the Epilogue at the end of the book.

# 19

# Sex Apart from Marriage

Fred is a twenty-one-year-old single Christian man who has come to see you for counseling. He reports struggling with sexual integrity. Here is his story told in his own words.

"I don't know what to do. Suzy is the first person I have ever dated. I wanted to do the right thing, and I wanted to be sure, so I spent months praying before I even asked her out on a date. We hit it off well from the start. We seemed to have a lot in common, and we connected emotionally. It definitely helped that we were friends for some time before we started dating. Our relationship progressed nicely as I tried to apply all the knowledge about dating that I had. I also had a good guy friend who I shared things with and was accountable to. Probably a month or so into our relationship, Suzy confessed her sexual sins that she committed in her past. Honestly, I was pretty hurt because her sexual experiences occurred at the same time that I had been praying whether to date her or not. I desired to be Godly and choose to forgive her. I also understood sexual sin. Ever since I was a teenager, I struggled with viewing sexual material and masturbating as a way to deal with my feelings of depression. I often felt alone and hurt because my parents neglected my emotional needs and were verbally abusive to me at times. Even though I was a Christian, sex seemed to fill the love that I longed for that my parents did not give me. This struggle increased dramatically when I went to college and had access to the Internet for the first time in my life. With easy access to the Internet, there were days when I spent enormous amounts of time looking at sexually explicit material and masturbating. I knew that what I was doing was wrong, and I would try to confess this to God and others. In knowing how much I struggled sexually, how could I not forgive Suzy?

"Probably less than a month into our relationship, Suzy and I were lying on the couch together late at night in her apartment. One thing led to another, and we began to get more sexual with each other. I had read in a Christian magazine about a couple who did not kiss until they got married, and I was very determined that this was the standard of purity that I wanted to uphold in my relationship with Suzy. Ironically, that night we engaged in a lot of sexual activity very quickly, and one of the last things we did was kiss. We felt extremely guilty, and I called my accountability partner the next day to confess all that I had done. I felt like such a failure because I was the man and was supposed to be the leader in the relationship. Suzy and I were so traumatized we even discussed breaking up. We continued our relationship, however. Suzy sought accountability for herself, I continued being accountable to my Christian brother, and Suzy and I both read books on how to maintain sexual purity. In addition, Suzy and I were both committed Christians, and we were even involved in a large student ministry at our college. I felt like we tried a lot of things, but we still had trouble not being involved sexually with each other. To add to our struggles of desiring to be sexually pure was my struggle to forgive her for her past sexual sins. I had thought that if I asked her a lot of questions and knew about her past in great detail, it would be better for me because then I would be able to forgive her more completely. On the contrary, I kept having thoughts of her being sexual with someone else and not me. I felt like such a hypocrite and hated myself. I struggled with my own sexual sins, but I could not forgive someone else. Our attempts to avoid being sexual with each other eventually worsened to the point where we had sexual intercourse one night and lost our virginity to each other. We tried breaking up at times, but to be honest, I couldn't handle it. I remember times where I felt incredibly abandoned and alone when we had tried to break up.

"Eventually, I increased the number of accountability partners I had from one to two, and I shared with various ministry leaders, friends, and pastors. I was desperate for help. After months of accountability, my accountability partners lovingly gave me the option of breaking up with Suzy or ending the accountability. I chose Suzy, and, honestly, our sexual struggles did not seem to change even without the accountability in my life. Outside of accountability, I also tried talking to several pastors. The first pastor I talked to listened to my story, shared some aspects of his life, and hypothesized that I was struggling sexually because I had a bad relationship with my father. He then invited me to pray, and after praying aloud together, he told me that I was not praying honestly because I was not praying with anger towards God. I was confused because I was not angry towards God, but I pondered his words and felt like I had been praying incorrectly my entire life. After our meeting, I prayed a lot and eventually decided against his advice of breaking up with Suzy. Months later, I talked to a second pastor, and he shared with me that he too had struggled with being sexual in his dating relationships. He admitted that having been married recently, he was still unsure of what he could have done differently in his past. I felt that, despite his uncertainty of knowing how to help me, this second pastor cared and even tried calling to check up on me one time. He also told me that if I ever figured out what to do in my situation, I should tell him because he was not quite sure himself. The third pastor I talked to I had known the longest and had the closest relationship with among all the pastors I had approached for help. He empathized with me as I told him my struggles, he talked about the challenges of being sexually pure in a dating relationship, and I cried as I experienced both his grace and my brokenness. I really felt like all three pastors cared for me and wanted my best, but for some reason I felt like the third pastor somehow was able to handle the enormity of my sexual sins. I am still struggling with being sexually pure with Suzy, forgiving her of her past, and not using Internet pornography. I really desire to be Godly, but I feel like I don't deserve God's love because of my past and continual sexual sins. I am here because this third pastor referred me to come see you. Please help me."

## Discussion Questions

1. How will you help Fred? What might be your approach?
2. What do you think might have caused Fred's problems with

lack of self-control? How would your answer influence your counseling?

3.  Would you urge Fred to break up with Suzy? Why or why not?

4.  Apparently Fred has not been helped by prayer, Scripture reading, and confessing to God or pouring out his heart to accountability partners. What *will* help?

5.  Unlike Fred, many people find accountability to be helpful in their struggles to control sexual thoughts and behaviors. What are reasons why accountability was not effective with Fred? Was the lack of effectiveness due to Fred, the accountability partners, or a combination of both? Give reasons for your answer. What would you recommend to make accountability more effective?

6.  What might be the long-term effects of Fred's sexual behavior and struggles? How can these adverse influences be prevented?

## General Questions

1.  Fred's struggles are not unusual. How could you help others to control themselves sexually?

2.  Assume that you are invited, as a counselor, to address a youth group in a church. What would you say about sexual purity?

3.  Assume that the invitation comes from a public school where you are not able to talk about religion. What would you say to this group? Your answers to this and the previous question may re-appear sometime when you are counseling with a counselee about sex within marriage.

4.  Would you predict that Fred's sexual struggles will disappear when and if he gets married? Give reasons for your answer. There is ample evidence that people who have difficulty with sexual control before marriage often have similar struggles after they are married. How could this be prevented for Fred?

## Personal Reflection Questions

1.  Think about your own sexuality. In what ways are you the same as Fred? In what ways are you different? How are you keeping sexual purity in your own life? If you are struggling

like Fred or Suzy is struggling, are you in any position to help? These are confidential questions, not to be discussed in class or with people you don't know or trust. Write about these issues in your journal or talk about them with somebody you respect and can trust to keep your conversation confidential. Understanding and controlling your sexuality will be important if you are to understand and help a counselee like Fred.

2. We live in a world where sex apart from marriage is widely accepted and not condemned, even in some church circles. Do you ever wonder if sexual purity is worth the effort? Why should Fred, or you, keep sexual purity? Can you give good reasons? Once again, keep your answers private, discussed only with a trusted friend or sensitive counselor.

3. Which of the three pastors, if any, is like you? What is the evidence that you will counsel Fred better than any of the pastors?

For a follow-up to the story of Fred, please go to the Epilogue at the end of the book.

# 20

# Sex Within Marriage

In their excellent book *When Two Become One*, Christopher and Rachel McCluskey write about enhancing sexual intimacy in marriage. "There is a world of difference between having sex and making love," the McCluskeys write. "Much more than just completing the conjugal act, making love is about enhancing a couple's experience of love on all planes of their relationship and having their sexual union be the truest expression of that love. Jesus constantly challenged us to examine the spirit of an act. The spirit of making love in Christian marriage, bonding spirit to spirit, soul to soul, body to body in three-dimensional union, is entirely different from simply having sex." In the case that follows, a couple appears to be more concerned about techniques for having sex than about the larger issues of intimacy in their relationship.

John and Brenda were the seemingly perfect Christian couple. John had been raised in a very affluent family that had made a fortune building commercial buildings. Brenda was an extremely bright educator whose intellect was only surpassed by her grace and compassion. They prayed together often, read Christian books, were leaders in their church, and volunteered to greet people when they arrived on Sunday mornings. Everything in their lives seemed to be going so well that initially it was unclear why they had come for counseling. That is, until John responded to a question about their sexual life together.

When the counselor asked if their sexual life was mutually satisfying, John replied, "I enjoy it, but she's such a prude." Brenda immediately burst into tears as she described feeling "completely unable" to satisfy John's sexual appetite. When encouraged to talk more about their sexual disconnect, Brenda stated that she was uncomfortable with John's sexual preferences and was not even sure that it was "OK" to do some of the things he enjoyed. John enjoyed some rather surprising sexual activities for a sixty-year-old. He tried to talk Brenda into experimenting with different sexual positions, liked to "role-play" and use sex toys, and often asked Brenda to engage in different forms of sex, including oral and anal sex. He liked to watch pornographic movies as a couple and try to repeat what they had seen on the screen. Brenda stated that she was unsure whether she enjoyed experimenting with John's "bag of tricks." While she did feel like some of John's desires were perhaps "sinful," she did find herself enjoying their exotic encounters at times. Regardless of whether Brenda was "OK" or not with their sex life, she was confident that she was not capable of satisfying his sexual desires. "The more I give in to him, the more he wants," she said toward the end of their first session.

John's sexual history included a number of interesting stories. His first sexual encounter was as a sixteen-year-old high school boy. In college he had become much more active sexually and had sex with many women before he met Brenda at age twenty-four. John estimated that he had slept with approximately seventy-five women before he was married. Although he clearly was a ladies' man earlier in life, he reported that he had been faithful to Brenda throughout their married life and that he didn't struggle with impure sexual thoughts or impulses toward other women.

When compared to her husband, Brenda's sexual experience before her marriage had been limited. Although she was not a virgin when she met John at twenty-two, she had only been with one other man. It is important to note that Brenda reported some sexual abuse by her uncle when she was around eight years old. She did not disclose this abuse when she was a child, and did not have much memory of the actual abuse experience.

When asked about their goals for counseling, John and Brenda stated that they would like clarity on God's view of their sex life in general, and on things like anal sex, sex toys, and watching pornographic movies in particular. They would like you to help them.

## Discussion Questions

1. What would be your approach in helping this couple? What counseling methods might you use?
2. What do you think may have caused the sexual problems that John and Brenda are having?
3. What, if any, is the evidence that John may struggle with a sexual addiction? Why might it be important to know if this is true? How would you find out?
4. In what ways may his rather extensive sexual history be an indication that he may have sexual issues that he has not mentioned?
5. Brenda is not sure if she enjoys some of the sexual experiences she has with John. Would you try to help Brenda better understand her own sexual needs and desires? Give reasons for your answer.
6. To what extent might the abuse be influencing Brenda's sexual attitudes?
7. Remember that the couple came to get answers to questions about their own sexual activities. Would you focus primarily on this request or would you explore other issues, such as those mentioned in the previous four questions? What would be reasons for dealing with these other issues? What would be reasons for staying with the question that John and Brenda asked?
8. The *Christian Counseling* book describes the DEC-R model of sexual counseling. How would you apply this to John and Brenda?

## General Questions

1. What does the Bible say about sex within marriage? Is it "OK" to engage in activities like oral and anal sex, the use of sex toys, and watching sexually explicit, arousing videos?
2. How could you help married couples set boundaries on what they do or do not do sexually?
3. In what ways would the age, gender, and marital status of the counselor impact counseling with John and Brenda? For

example, are there reasons why a single male counselor in his twenties would have a different influence on this couple than, say, a middle-aged female counselor who is married? Are there other kinds of counselors who would or would not be effective in working with John and Brenda? Give reasons for your answer.

### Personal Reflection Questions

1. Has discussion of the case of John and Brenda left you feeling uncomfortable in any way? Can you think of reasons for your answer? With what trusted person could you discuss your discomforts in a way that lets you be honest and feel accepted? What would be the reasons for this discussion?

2. Considering your age, marital status, training, and sexual experience, would you be willing to help a couple like John and Brenda? What might make you feel reluctant to help them? What would be reasons that you would go ahead and work with them as their counselor? Now is a good time to think through these questions (perhaps with the help of a trusted friend and/or a counselor) and not later when you are in the counseling room with a couple like John and Brenda waiting for your response to questions about sex.

3. What kind of extra training might you need to do sex counseling? Where would you get this training? (The web site that accompanies this book and the *Christian Counseling* book has some initial suggestions. See *www.garyrcollins.com*.)

For a follow-up to the story of John and Brenda, please go to the Epilogue at the end of the book.

# 21

# Homosexuality

Christian psychologist John Court has written that homosexual acts have been recorded throughout history, but these "do not assume a lifetime orientation or even a predominant attraction to the same sex. No society in history has endorsed adult homosexual relationships of the kind advocated today. Evidence of exclusive homosexuality has been sketchy, probably due to its rarity." Court adds that homosexual behavior "appears in the New Testament among catalogs of sins without any indication that it is more heinous than lying or greediness." Even so, evidences of homosexuality can create great tensions in the church, in families, and in the individuals involved. The two cases that follow describe (1) a teenager whose concerns about gender identity brought her to a counselor and (2) a youth leader in his twenties whose feelings of attraction toward other males greatly impacted his life and his ministry.

## CASE STORY 1—Julia

Identity development during adolescence can be a time of intense stress and confusion. This is seen in Julia, age sixteen, who has professed Jesus Christ as her Lord and Savior and who is active in her church youth group. She is not from a strong Christian family but asked her parents to take her to a Christian counselor so she could talk about a deep inner struggle and long-term shame. With honesty and courage, Julia told her story, then she faced the counselor squarely, made direct eye contact, and posed the question that had been concerning her: "Am I gay?"

This opened a long conversation regarding her fears, fantasies, future, family expectations, and faith. She described several times when she felt sexual attraction to peers of the same sex, but she added that she does find some of her male peers "cute" and "great." Julia has never had a serious boyfriend, but she does have male friends who discuss their problems with her. Several years ago (at age twelve or thirteen), she became aware that she had feelings and maybe an attraction toward a female who was part of her close friendship group. She reported that there were times when she wanted to kiss her friend, hug her, and be really close to her. Julia added that these feelings toward her friend may have been romantic and perhaps even sexual.

On a recent youth retreat, Julia was placed in the same room with a girl that was a newcomer to the group. The two developed such a close connection that, by the end of the weekend, they felt like old friends and the other girl mentioned that it was "weird" how they had grown so close so quickly. It was as if they "fell in love at first sight." The use of that phrase bothered Julia. She has been fearful about continuing this friendship now that the retreat has ended, but Julia admits to thinking about this girl, having weird thoughts, and noticing strange bodily sensations.

Concerning her background, Julia had a fairly uneventful upbringing and comes from an intact family that has lived in the same community for her entire life. There is a younger brother who is her "father's favorite" according to Julia. At school, she is an average student but good at soccer (her position is goalie), and this gets attention from her father, who loves this sport. She is physically strong, solidly built, not stocky but muscular. She is "big boned" according to her mother's description.

When asked about any sexual history, she reported that the memories are vague. She does recall some childhood sexual play with peers around the year that she started school, and she remembers seeing another girl naked along with a neighborhood boy.

There was no abuse associated with these memories. When she was in second or third grade, an older boy (young teen) did approach her sexually. He touched her in her private areas over her clothing and overrode her protests. He also exposed himself to her but warned her to be quiet about this. For Julia, this was a brief but traumatic experience that was frightening. She did not tell her parents right away, but she cried so much at home that her mother got the story out of her. The boy's family was apparently confronted by both of her parents, but nothing more was ever said about it and Julia was told by her mother not to tell anyone about the incident. Her parents believed her, but they wanted the whole matter kept quiet. No other remarkable sexual experiences were reported.

The parents are immigrants from Eastern Europe who came to the United States from a communist country when they were very young. They are hard working but do not seem to have a close marriage and do not spend much time together. The family attends soccer games and goes to school events, but they do not appear to be connected to the community, have no relatives in the area, and are only nominal Christians. When they wanted to come to America, a Christian group helped to facilitate the move and provided them with assistance when they arrived. A local church helped the father find employment, enabled the family to get an apartment, and eventually gave them a financial gift to help buy their first home. The parents are very indebted to this conservative evangelical church, but attending services is a low priority. Julia does not report any meaningful signs of a Christian life at home. She has never heard her father pray, and the Bibles in the house are more for show than for reading. In fact, her father is never seen reading, and this has made Julia wonder if he really can read.

The parents are skeptical of counseling but are disturbed enough to set up the first appointment. The big questions on their minds appear to be "What did we do wrong?" "Did something happen to make our daughter this way?" and "Will we ever have grandchildren?" Julia would very much like to have her question answered.

## Discussion Questions

1. How will you deal with the parents' questions that appear in the final paragraph?
2. How will you answer Julia's question, "Am I gay?" Give reasons for your answer.

3. What would be your counseling goals with this family? Why have you chosen these goals and not others?

4. Describe the approach you will take in your counseling with Julia.

5. What may have caused Julia's sexual orientation? How would your answers to this question be used in your counseling with Julia and her family?

6. Julia is a Christian. How would you utilize Christian, biblical principles in your work with Julia and/or her family?

## General Questions

1. As part of their identity development, for a time many teenagers feel sexual attractions both to same-sex and to opposite-sex peers. Give reasons why Julia's attraction to other girls is no more than a normal part of growing up. Give reasons why there may be a more long-term same-sex orientation in Julia.

2. Assume that you are Julia's counselor. Will you include the parents or not include them in the counseling sessions? Give reasons why it might be best to counsel Julia privately without her parents. Give reasons for including the parents in your counseling sessions.

## Personal Reflection Questions

Please see the end of this chapter for *Personal Reflection Questions.*

## CASE STORY 2—Billy

For several years Billy has been the youth pastor at the biggest church in a small town in the southern United States. Almost everybody knows Billy. At least they think they do. But Billy is hiding a huge secret from all the students in his youth ministry, from all the parents of the kids he works with, and especially from the rest of the pastoral staff. That's why Billy was so concerned about confidentiality when he came to his first counseling session. He spent about fifteen minutes at the beginning questioning the counselor in multiple ways about whether he would ever tell anyone the content of their sessions. After he was reassured that the counselor only broke confidentiality in order to keep people safe, Billy leaned forward and said softly, "OK, I guess I'm ready to do this." And he told his secret.

Billy feels sexually attracted to other guys. He has never had sex with a man or looked at homosexual pornography, but Billy stated that he sometimes feels an overwhelming desire to be around other men that he views as more powerful or attractive than he is. He added that he was very embarrassed by the fact that he would sometimes get aroused "just looking" at a man. For instance, Billy has a hard time working out at the gym because he will sometimes get an erection as he watches other guys working out. Billy also told the counselor about feeling very excited by thoughts of the male genitalia, even if this was not connected to any man in particular. Body parts, as he put it, are very stimulating. Obviously, Billy doesn't want to have these sexual thoughts and feelings, and he is very much afraid that someone will find out about his same-sex attraction. Ironically, Billy also said that he does not feel like he is gay. He stated that he has no interest in having sex with a man, and he doesn't feel as though he would ever be interested in homosexual activities. In fact, he said that he wants very much to marry a woman one day.

Billy grew up with seven sisters in a rural town in Louisiana. His mother was very overbearing, but extremely attentive to her son. In some ways, the atmosphere in his family of origin was like a sorority. He described scantily clad sisters who would laugh and play around him, and a mother who would bathe in front of him until he went to college. Obviously, modesty wasn't a strong trait in his family—except in the case of Billy's father. He was described as a fine Christian man who took his faith seriously. But as smothering as Billy's mother was at times, his father was just as disconnected. Although he couldn't really describe any fond memories about times with his dad as a child, Billy said that he always liked his dad. In fact, Billy said that he had often wanted to spend more time with his dad, but the father typically was preoccupied with other activities like reading or chores. All in all, Billy reported that as he looked back on his childhood he remembered feeling like most of the family's activities focused on making his mother happy.

Sexually, Billy had a rather nondescript experience growing up.

Excluding the unusual exposure Billy had to the female body in his family of origin, he has had limited experience with women. He dated one girl all three years of high school and had one girlfriend in college. Not surprisingly, his college sweetheart was very endearing, dramatic, and needy. Although this girl was very attractive, Billy never felt sexually interested. He said that they did "fool around" several times, but he was never able to achieve an erection when he was with her. Accordingly, Billy was still a virgin who was committed to finding a girl whom he could connect with sexually once they were married. In the meantime, he wanted to be free from his same-sex attractions, but he wondered if counseling could really help.

### Discussion Questions

1. Do you think counseling will help? Give reasons for your answer.
2. How would you counsel Billy? What would be your counseling goals?
3. In commenting on this case, Billy's counselor wrote the following: "I struggled with how to treat Billy. He didn't accept the title of 'gay,' but he was obviously more attracted to men than to women. Should the treatment have been behavioral in nature, which would focus on untangling the sexual response Billy had to the male body? Or should counseling be more psychodynamic in nature, which would address the underlying family issues that seemed to drive Billy's attraction to men? Should the focus be on helping Billy apply biblical guidelines on homosexuality to his life?" How would you help the counselor with his dilemma of knowing how to treat Billy? Which approach would you take? Why?
4. The counselor in this case also "struggled with the extent to which it was necessary for Billy to admit that he was attracted to men and that he obviously was interested in homosexual sex. Was he repressing his desire to have sex with men, and would it be necessary for him to confront that desire and to admit it honestly in order to be free from its bondage?" Do you think Billy needs to admit some things that he appears to be denying? What are these things? Why might it be necessary for

him to admit them? Are there reasons why admitting them would not be helpful?

5. What are the causes of Billy's sexual orientation? What is the role of his mother, his sisters, his father? How can this knowledge be used in the counseling?

## General Questions

1. In your opinion, can a person who is sexually attracted to members of his or her own sex change that orientation? Give reasons for your answer.

2. Summarize the biblical teaching about homosexuality. How does this apply to Julia and her family? How does this apply to Billy and his work as a youth minister?

3. Is it important to counsel Billy to step down from his position until he has cleared up his own sexual identity? Is he putting himself (and others) at risk by being in a position of authority over young men when he is unsure of why and how he is attracted to certain men? If you encourage him to resign, how will this impact Billy, his family, his youth group, and his church?

4. What might be reasons for Billy to stay in his position? Would you recommend that he resign or remain where he is? Give reasons for your decision.

## Personal Reflection Questions

1. Privately, give some thought to your own sexual orientation. To what extent are you attracted sexually to people of your own gender? You may want to write answers in a journal, but be sure that this journal is kept in a place where others would not read it. Should you talk with somebody about your own sexual attractions? If so, who would you talk to? How would you know that confidentiality would be maintained? Why would you talk about this with a close friend or counselor?

2. How do you personally react to the biblical teaching about homosexuality? How does this apply to you and to your sexual identity?

3. Homophobia has been defined as an emotional response to homosexual people or to homosexuality characterized by "un-Christian acts of denial, rejection, discrimination, contempt, hostility, or violence toward homosexuals." Are you homophobic? Be honest. Ask somebody who knows you well if you show evidence of homophobia. If so, how can this change in you? Remember, even if one believes homosexual behavior is morally wrong, the Christian still can and should treat homosexual people, like Julia or Billy, in gracious and supportive ways.

4. Who is your closest friend or relative? Think of a specific person. Now assume that your closest friend or relative admits to you that he or she is gay. How will you react? What does this say about you? What does this say about how you might counsel people who struggle with sexual-orientation issues?

For a follow-up to the stories of Julia and Billy, please go to the Epilogue at the end of the book.

# Abuse and Neglect

Childhood sexual abuse impacts countless individuals and often leads to severe developmental problems. When a survivor of childhood sexual abuse reaches adulthood without treatment, he or she often has internalized a sense of inferiority and shame. This can have detrimental effects on the person's relationships, career functioning, and ability to develop a coherent sense of self. As you read the story of Ms. K, think about how you would understand her struggles and how you might best approach treatment to help her.

Ms. K is a twenty-five-year-old, single female who has been employed as a kindergarten teacher since her graduation from college. She is a member of a local church, where she is actively involved in volunteer work and connected to a small group of close friends from college. Ms. K sought counseling upon the urging of a concerned older friend and mentor. She came with hesitation, however, because she had been guarded and hesitant to participate fully when others had pressured her to go for counseling in the past.

Ms. K grew up in a pastor's home. The family moved several times during her childhood as her father took new church placements. Her immediate family consisted of her parents, herself, and an older brother (Damon)—who came to be her primary abuser.

Looking back, Ms. K can admit that she did not feel safe sharing her fears at home, let alone disclosing the ongoing abuse by her brother. She describes her father as having two personalities—public and private. Although he would be described by his church congregations as cheerful, humorous, and committed to serving others, at home he has always been strict, short-tempered, and controlling. Even now, as an adult, Ms. K is intimidated by her father's personality when she visits home and struggles when observing his winsome public persona. Her mother is described as one who would work hard to please the father, urging the children to accommodate his needs when he came home tired in the evenings. The mother was critical of her daughter, intolerant of the children's imperfections, but passive with her husband. Ms. K remembers feeling the pressure of trying to please her father but never feeling that she could do anything right. This sense of never doing anything right is one she carries with her today. As a pastor's child in a conservative church denomination, she also grew up believing that as a human being she is wholly sinful and bad, undeserving of any good thing. In the context of her abuse, this theological belief became distorted to the point of believing that she deserved the abuse that was inflicted upon her.

Ms. K is eight years younger than her brother. Because of this age difference, he often was placed in a position of authority over her by the parents, was often asked to be her babysitter on weekend evenings, or was expected to watch her after school until their parents came home from work. It was during these times and with this position of power that Damon came to expect the sister to perform sexual acts with him. Damon was viewed by his family, teachers, and church communities as a charming, respectful, and responsible adolescent. He always was the brother, cousin, or peer that other youth looked up to with admiration.

Damon's abuse began when Ms. K was six years old. The brother described his initial approaches as "games," in which he would dare her to reveal herself or touch him in ways that at first seemed playful and then became progressively more uncomfortable. These "games" quickly progressed within a few months to forced oral sex and then to vaginal penetration. Abuse incidents were described as frequent, often several times a week, and lasting for a duration of six years. During those years, Ms. K came to believe that she was a willing participant, an equal partner in the sexual activity, despite the fact that the incidents were usually verbally demeaning and abusive. Ms. K remembers being silenced any time she would cry out in pain. Damon would cover her mouth with his hand or with a pillow. Even today she shudders with fear at the memory of being trapped and smothered.

During her early adolescent years, when the abuse began to taper off due to her brother's absence from the home, Ms. K began to develop more of a realization of what had happened to her, and with that realization came an increasing sense of shame. To deal with the vivid memories and nightmares that began to haunt her, Ms. K began cutting herself with a razor to temporarily alleviate her stress. She described this act as "a pain I could choose and control," and as an adult she continues to periodically lapse back into self-harm when overwhelmed. Toward the end of her adolescent years, shortly before leaving for college, Ms. K's secret was revealed to her parents against her will after she confided in a friend who felt the need to disclose the issue to a trusted teacher. The teacher knew that she had a legal responsibility to tell the authorities.

This was a painful time in life as Ms. K's private pain and shame suddenly were revealed to those who did not protect her as a child. In the following weeks the parents confronted Damon, but overall their daughter's experience was emotionally minimized and there was rampant denial regarding the long-term effects of this severe abuse. The issue was not discussed in the family past the initial month, and there was an unspoken message which persists into the present, that Ms. K could "get on with life" now that the issue has been "dealt with." The father told Ms. K that Damon was "repentant" of his sins in the past, but Damon has never discussed this directly with his sister. The brother was encouraged to get help if needed, but apparently he never did so. There were no legal ramifications of his actions, and presently Damon serves both as a middle school teacher and a leader in his church. The family continues to gather together for holidays, and there is an expectation that both adult children will visit home regularly and as often as possible.

Currently, Ms. K's symptoms would best fit the diagnostic criteria of chronic post-traumatic stress disorder, with bouts of major depression. She experiences nightmares and intrusive memories of the past which will leave her shaken for hours or days following each episode. Probably most destructive, however, are the thoughts about herself as dirty, inferior to normal people, and undeserving of a fulfilling life.

She has struggled with suicidal thoughts periodically, and has profound questions about her faith in a God who is sovereign, yet allowed this childhood nightmare to continue for so many years.

## Discussion Questions

1. Assume that you are Ms. K's counselor. She has come at the urging of a friend, but she is hesitant to participate fully. With this knowledge, how would you approach the counseling? What would you do to reassure Ms. K so that she is encouraged to stay in the counseling relationship?
2. The *Christian Counseling* book discusses reasons for abuse. What are the causes of the abuse in Ms. K's life? When these causes are identified, how can this knowledge be of value in counseling Ms. K?
3. In what ways has the abuse influenced Ms. K's life? Be specific.
4. What is the evidence that she is angry? Do you think it is important to focus on this anger (if it exists) and help Ms. K deal with these feelings? Give reasons for your answer. How would you help her deal with this anger?
5. The story of Ms. K does not mention forgiveness. To fully recover from her abuse does she need to forgive her brother and her parents? Give reasons for your answer. Do the family members need to ask her for forgiveness? Can she "get on with life" if this forgiveness is not forthcoming?
6. What is the present impact of the abuse on Ms. K's self-concept?
7. Is it possible for Ms. K to have a healthy marriage in the future, including fulfilling sex with her husband? What might hinder this? What could you do to help the counselee prepare for marriage?

## General Questions

1. Give reasons why Ms. K should have a female counselor. Give reasons why her counselor should be male. Give reasons why the gender of the counselor would not matter in this case.
2. Summarize the ways in which counselors may be influenced by working with abuse victims and their perpetrators. Give

specific ways in which you can protect yourself from the harmful effects of working with people involved in abuse.

3. Do you think Damon needs counseling? If he came to you for counseling, how would you work with him?

4. Abuse is rampant, even in the Christian community according to some experts. As a counselor, what can you do to prevent abuse?

## Personal Reflection Questions

1. As you read the case of Ms. K, what feelings did you have concerning Damon, the parents, the parents' theology, and Ms. K? In what ways would feelings like this influence your counseling work with Ms. K or members of her family?

2. What is the evidence, if any, that you have been abused? How has this impacted you? How will it influence your work as a counselor? Write your answers in a journal, then discuss this privately with a counselor.

3. What is the evidence, if any, that you have abused some other person or persons? What can you do to bring healing in the other person and in yourself? Be specific.

For a follow-up to the story of Ms. K, please go to the Epilogue at the end of the book.

PART FIVE

---

# Identity Issues

# Inferiority and Self-Esteem

A graduate student recently sent an email message to one of his counseling professors. "I have always been challenged by my own doubts and insecurities," the student wrote. "So many men struggle with their own insecurities, and God has dealt with that in my life. I am telling you this, because this is me stepping out in a major way." Insecurity, inferiority, and self-esteem issues are not limited to counseling students or to men. This is a common problem that many people bring to counselors. Mrs. A is an example.

Mrs. A is a thirty-five-year-old married mother of three young children. She does not work outside the home, though in recent months she has taken on more responsibilities in the music ministry of their local congregation (a large, televised ministry). Her husband is a physician who specializes in difficult pediatric procedures. They are both strong believers, committed to Christ and to one another, though the original presenting problem for counseling was "marriage issues."

When she was growing up, Mrs. A reports that her parents were "wonderful," and that they provided an "almost perfect Christian home." Mrs. A's father was a well-known pastor and her mother a stay-at-home mom who "really focused on making a home for us." Upon further exploration it became clear that Mrs. A's father expected the children to be perfect because "people are watching." The mother may have been charming at church, but at home she was emotionally distant and unable to focus on Mrs. A and her sister. Mrs. A grew up believing that her best never quite measured up, and she had no one to talk with about her fears. It became easier for her to anticipate criticism than to expect that her behavior might result in praise or affirmation, only to have those hopes destroyed by criticism and neglect. This pattern became so ingrained that Mrs. A began anticipating failure in almost every situation. That anticipation confused her: she knew that she could do things well, but she always expected to fail. It became safer for her to stay in the background, not make waves, and avoid the spotlight.

Despite her internal rule to avoid the spotlight, Mrs. A continued to long for both connection and achievement. Growing up in a home that valued accomplishment, she felt helpless, unable to achieve that which was still expected. Over time, Mrs. A became more and more frustrated because of her inability to please the people who mattered the most to her. Ironically, this frustration drove her to try even harder, further validating her confusion over who she really was. The scraps of approval that she occasionally gained from parents, teachers, or church leaders felt so life-giving to her that she continued to seek validation from sources external to her.

When she married, Mrs. A found a husband who was high-achieving and able to provide well for their family. However, despite early feelings of emotional connection, the husband appeared to have increasing difficulty expressing emotion. After several years of marriage and the birth of their two children, the interchanges between Dr. and Mrs. A had come to resemble something similar to her early upbringing. Her attempts to gain intimacy from her husband resulted in swings of neediness and anger, which caused further tension between them.

By the time they came for counseling, Mrs. A's misery had grown and the interactions with her husband were leading to increasing insecurity and feelings of inferiority.

## Discussion Questions

1.  Summarize the causes of Mrs. A's inferiority feelings. What is she doing to maintain these feelings? What might be reasons for her attempts to maintain her low self-esteem?
2.  Do you see ambivalence in Mrs. A? Describe this.

3. What approach would you take in your work with Mrs. A and her husband? Give reasons for your answer.

4. What might be some goals in counseling?

5. Mrs. A appears to be in a cycle. She wants and tries to succeed. She expects to fail. When she fails, the cycle is repeated as she tries again to succeed. How could this cycle be broken?

6. As a Christian counselor, how might your approach in this case differ from that of a counselor who is not Christian? How would your approach be similar to what might be used by a secular counselor?

## General Questions

1. What "causes" inferiority? Why do individuals who feel inferior keep finding people or putting themselves into situations that perpetuate the feelings of inferiority and low self-esteem? What is the evidence for this in Mrs. A?

2. What are biblical concepts that relate to inferiority and low self-esteem? Which of these biblical truths could apply to Mrs. A? What is the evidence that it would be difficult to apply these truths to Mrs. A?

3. How would you use biblical concepts without further stimulating Mrs. A's ambivalence?

4. What is the likelihood that the family's two daughters will develop low self-esteem and inferiority like their mother? How can this be prevented?

5. When counselors feel insecure and inferior, how does this impact their counseling work?

## Personal Reflection Questions

1. This chapter began with the words of a counseling student who wrote that "I have always been challenged by my own doubts and insecurities." To what extent is that true of you? How have your insecurities influenced your life? Write your responses in a journal that you can keep in a secure place. Who can you talk with about your own insecurities?

2. How do your own insecurities influence your counseling? How

can these insecurities be prevented from hindering your work as a counselor?

3.  In what ways do the life, attitudes, and experiences of Mrs. A describe you as well? How could a counselor be of help to you?

4.  The student at the beginning of the chapter wrote that talking about his insecurities was a major step forward and that God was helping the student deal with the self-doubts and insecurities. How is God working with the insecurities in your life? How could you be more receptive to his influence?

For a follow-up to the story of Mrs. A, please go to the Epilogue at the end of the book.

# 24

# Physical Illness

Unlike some of the problems in this book, physical illness comes to all of us at times. Sickness is little more than an annoyance if it comes in the form of a cold or flu and disappears after a few days. When the illness persists, however, it can have a radical impact on our lives and on the people around us. To illustrate the physical, psychological, and spiritual impact of chronic illness, I have chosen the case of a young man whose physical problems began at about the time he was starting school.

When he was six years old, Paul was diagnosed with juvenile rheumatoid arthritis (JRA) in his left knee. Nobody in his family or at the school had heard of this illness, but after taking Paul to several perplexed doctors, they soon learned that JRA is an autoimmune disease in which the body perceives certain joints as foreign objects and attempts to remove them. This can be extremely painful as swelling occurs and the body goes about eating up its own joints.

A painful illness can be difficult to bear even when there is support from friends and family, but Paul did not have this support. His parents did not get along with each other and were largely absent from his life. After they divorced, when Paul was eight years old, he and his sisters continued living with the mother who, once or twice a year, would show "rare compassionate attention" (Paul's words) and would take her son to see the rheumatologist. This doctor regularly tried new drugs in an attempt to control the JRA. At one time he called to say that Paul's blood work showed that the prescribed dosage was far too high and that he should be hospitalized. "He's fine," the mother responded. "He's outside hauling wood in the snow right now." But the pain continued, and occasionally Paul would undergo the painful procedure of having his knee drained and injected with steroids.

When Paul was twelve years old his mother remarried, gave birth to another child, and moved to another city all in the same week. The new stepfather was an abusive, unpredictable alcoholic who created stress for the whole family. Stress greatly impacts the intensity of JRA, so perhaps it is not surprising that from this point the disease began to spread very quickly. When he was in junior high and high school, there were times when Paul would wake up in the morning and the pain and swelling in his joints would be so bad that he could not walk. Despite the discomfort in his left knee, Paul had always been active. He still is. He had enjoyed wrestling since he was about six, but at age sixteen he knew he had to quit the team when during a practice the pain became so bad that he could not walk." I'm not sure that I thought of asking someone to help me," Paul wrote after reading this paragraph. "I still remember that sad day pretty clearly, supporting myself fully with my arms on the hand rails as I went up the stairs, almost dragging my legs behind me, fighting back tears and feeling very alone. The reason I didn't ask for help was likely because I did not want to appear weak and also because I grew up not having parents to ask for help. I had to figure out how to take care of myself."

By this time, among other drugs, Paul was taking Methotrexate, which is more commonly used at higher doses for chemotherapy. The drug would make him nauseous when taken orally, so at age eighteen he asked if he could inject the drug, hoping to prevent the gagging. Unfortunately, this did not help; the psychosomatic reaction had become so great that just thinking about the medication would cause a nauseous gagging reaction. All of this led Paul to imagine the negative impact that a few decades of consuming poisonous drugs could have on his body, so he researched many naturopathic means for addressing the disease, even as it continued to get worse. At twenty he stopped taking prescribed medications and made great sacrifices to use only naturopathic remedies. Some of these helped address the disease, but it continued to get worse and at a faster rate. By this time the disease had spread to almost every joint in his body. Paul's hands, wrists, ankles, feet, jaw, knees, chest, and shoulders were painful, swollen, and deteriorating. Moving was extremely painful. Every step had to be planned to minimize pain. A year or so later he began taking Methotrexate again, but the disease was still devouring his body. The constant piercing and exhausting pain begin wearing him down, and on one extremely painful day he staggered slowly from the couch to draw a hot bath. He sat in the water wishing he could die—wishing he believed in suicide. The tears flowed freely as he wept over the pain and hopelessness of a body that was continuing to painfully consume itself, even after he had tried virtually every medication, naturopathic remedy, and prayer available. It seemed that things only would get worse as his joints fused together and Paul would live in utter agony. He didn't even have the hope of taking his own life to end the pain.

## Discussion Questions

1. Assume that Paul's doctor is concerned about his depression and thoughts of suicide, so the doctor refers him to you for counseling. Where would you begin?

2. In addition to Paul's physical illness, what others issues and stresses are contributing to his physical condition and personal struggles? How will you deal with these?

3. Where is the evidence that Paul has social support to help him cope? How would you help him find additional support that is healthy?

4. The *Christian Counseling* book discusses some common reactions that are seen in people with physical illnesses. These reactions include denial, defensiveness, withdrawal, anxiety, anger, and manipulation of other people. Which of these do you see in Paul? How would you deal with these? How would you determine if these are reactions that may be putting stress on Paul even if he hasn't expressed them?

5. Suppose that Paul raises some difficult questions about his illness, including the following. How would you help his deal with each of these?
   - Why is this happening to me?
   - Why is God allowing this?

- Do the doctors really know what they are doing?
- Why has God not healed me?
- Does God care about this suffering?

## General Questions

1.  Counselors are hope-givers. What hope can you give Paul? Can you give hope to him if you do not feel this hope in yourself?
2.  Researchers and pain-management specialists have developed techniques for helping people manage pain psychologically. Take a few minutes to look up some of these methods on the Internet. How might these help Paul?
3.  Would part of your treatment involve helping Paul develop work skills so he could maintain employment? Give reasons for your answer. How would you help him develop these skills?
4.  Paul is a Christian, but this was never mentioned in the case story except for the reference to prayer. What biblical and other Christian principles would you bring into your counseling? How would you introduce these?
5.  Assume that Paul might be angry with God because he has allowed his suffering. In what ways will you help Paul with his anger? What will you do if he does not want to talk about God or about anything religious?
6.  Paul does not have a very supportive family. Suppose he did have a family who cared. How would you help the family?
7.  If the opportunity for discussion ever arose, how would you help Paul's doctor deal with the stresses of handling patients like this?

## Personal Reflection Questions

1.  What is your attitude toward people who are chronically ill and/or have severe physical limitations? Do you feel uncomfortable being with these people? Be honest: do you prefer to avoid these people? If so, what are the reasons for your feelings and attitudes? Is this evidence of prejudice in you? What is its origin? How can you feel more comfortable in the presence of people who suffer?

2. How will your attitudes toward people who suffer physically have an influence on how you counsel?

3. If you are a person who appears to have a special ability to relate to patients like Paul, how do you account for this perspective? How might God use this in your future counseling? What steps can you take to turn this asset into a means for helping others who suffer physically but also struggle psychologically, relationally, and spiritually?

For a follow-up to the story of Paul, please go to the Epilogue at the end of the book.

# 25

# Grief

Grief can occur in a variety of forms. There can be grieving over the loss of a job, relationship, opportunity, or valued possession. People grieve when they lose hope, a dream for the future, good health, a place of residence, or a pet. Similar principles of grieving can apply in all these situations, but by far the most often encountered grieving comes with the loss of a loved one who has died. This is the grief that a counselor saw in Mrs. M.

Mrs. M came into counseling six weeks after the loss of her husband. He had been on the police force for thirty years and had retired five years earlier, taking a part-time security job to stay active. His death was sudden and unexpected, but due entirely to natural causes. The couple had been married for forty-two years and had three adult sons, all of whom live some distance from Mrs. M. She and her husband had a very strong marriage with highly defined gender roles. Consequently, Mrs. M has found herself in an entirely new situation of having major financial and household responsibilities. Although her sons are concerned and anxious to be of assistance, they are not available on a daily basis. Mrs. M came in for counseling at the request of her sons, who feel that she may not be handling daily life well and are concerned for her grasp of reality. When she came for counseling, she was very open and admitted she was not sure she was coping well.

She related several incidents that were particularly troubling. Two involved having driven the car to a location and then, forgetting that she had the car, taking public transportation home. Her sons eventually brought the car home, although they were concerned about her forgetfulness. Several times she has locked herself out of the car and had to have one of her sons arrange for a locksmith to open the car door. The last time this happened she called a friend for assistance because she did not want her sons to know. One of the sons has helped her to get her own checking account and is handling all the large financial decisions. Nevertheless, she often feels uncertain in writing checks or dealing with financial issues.

The most recent significant incident was when she experienced an episode of such severe grief that she considered taking her own life. However, she dismissed the idea of suicide after a brief discussion with her pastor. Mrs. M said that she had been temporarily overwhelmed by all the changes and responsibilities but that such despair was not part of her basic personality. In addition she felt that upon reflection such an action would be both unfair to her sons and morally wrong. Mrs. M has attended a denominational church for many years and feels well connected there. Her friends from church have been of much assistance; however, she feels they are pushing her to make changes that she is not yet ready to make, such as changing furniture in her home or dealing with her husband's belongings.

While she currently denies any suicidal ideation, she is very troubled by the fact that she actually had any such thoughts and feels that if she told her sons they would be sure that she was losing her mind. They already were mentioning repeatedly the possibility of her moving in with one of them, although none was set up for that possibility. She prefers to remain independent and in her own home and community.

Mrs. M has come in to counseling struggling to define her new roles in life and to learn new skills. She expresses a desire to become more independent rather than transferring her dependence from her husband to her sons. She is upset that she often feels angry with her husband for taking such good care of her that she currently feels helpless without him.

## Discussion Questions

1. How do you evaluate Mrs. M's grief? In what ways is it healthy and normal; in what ways is it not?

2. Review the section titled "The Effects of Grief" in the *Christian Counseling* book. Which of these effects is Mrs. M. showing?

3. In what ways, if any, has the sudden nature of her husband's death contributed to Mrs. M's grieving?

4. Discuss the role of the sons. In what ways are they being helpful to Mrs. M? What problems might they be creating for her?

5. What will be your goals in counseling Mrs. M? What approaches to counseling will you take? Give reasons for your answers to both questions.

6. Based on what you have read, what recommendations will you make to the sons who referred Mrs. M to you?

7. Will you tell Mrs. M what evaluation and/or recommendations you plan to tell her sons? Give your reasons for and against telling her. Discuss the pros and cons of meeting with Mrs. M and her sons together and giving your recommendations to the whole family group.

## General Questions

1. How could Mrs. M's church be more helpful in her grieving process? What might be the role, positive and/or negative, of other widows making themselves available to give Mrs. M encouragement, guidance, and companionship when she needs it?

2. Think of a specific situation in which a person grieves the loss of an object, relationship, or situation other than the death of a loved one. The first paragraph in this chapter gives examples of grieving apart from a death. In what ways does your knowledge of the grieving process apply to the situation that has come to your mind?

3. What is complicated grief? How would you describe it to another person? In what specific ways can you prevent it?

4. We have read about Mrs. M's sons and friends, but where is Jesus in her grief? In what ways will you bring him into your counseling with this lady?

5. Make a prediction about the course of Mrs. M's grief if she (a) remains in her community and has counseling, (b) remains in her community but does not meet with a counselor, and/or (c) moves in with one of her sons.

## Personal Reflection Questions

1.  Probably it is true that most of us do not like to think about the death of a loved one. Have you thought about this? Write your reflections on this grief in a journal or other secure place. What are reasons why you do not like to think about grief? What are reasons why you should think about grieving in your own life?

2.  How will others respond when you die? Having thought about this, what behavior or attitude changes might you make in your life? When will you start? What will get in the way of making these changes? Who will hold you accountable?

3.  Are there ways in which you are like Mr. M had been—so involved in caring for his spouse that she felt helpless and angry after he had gone? How should you change?

4.  Give the reasons why you would be a good grief counselor. What is the evidence that you would not be a good grief counselor? What can you do now to be a better grief counselor in the future?

For a follow-up to the story or Mrs. M, please go to the Epilogue at the end of the book.

# Singleness

A significant proportion of the adult population is single, but many people find it very difficult to be unmarried in a world where most adults are married and where there is a widespread expectation that most normal people will get married. Despite these cultural attitudes, many single people adapt to their singleness and learn to live fulfilled lives. Others do not succeed so well. The story of Susan can help us understand and more effectively counsel people who are single, whether or not this is their choice.

Susan is a thirty-eight-year-old single woman who sought Christian counseling specifically because she felt confused and overwhelmed by her life. She is a middle manager for a large sales organization, well respected and moving ahead professionally in areas she generally enjoys. She admits that she works long hours and is often cited as a person who is dependable and a good manager because she will do whatever it takes to get the job done. She feels that because she does not have a husband or children, she should be more available than some of her married colleagues.

Although raised in a nominally Christian home, it was not until ten years ago that she became serious about spiritual things and started regularly attending church. Although not highly involved in the community life of the church, she regularly attends and enjoys the worship activities. Her Bible study and knowledge are growing, and her prayer life is strong. Although she enjoys the church, she does not feel strongly connected because of the heavy emphasis on marriage and family. She feels that as an older single professional woman she must work hard to build connections in the church. Women's ministries in her church tend to focus on motherhood and parenting stages. Usually the women's activities take place during the day to accommodate school schedules. Susan's heavy work schedule often precludes regular involvement with any type of fellowship group.

In her twenties and early thirties Susan had two serious relationships. The second one led to an engagement that lasted two months. Susan broke it off after finding that her fiancé was not entirely truthful with her and was continuing a close friendship with a former lover. She does not regret either relationship and clearly feels that both were appropriately ended. She has close friendships with a number of women through work-related activities, although none of the women is strongly Christian. Her family members are close, and she often finds herself in caretaking situations with them, particularly with her younger brother, who has been through a series of poor relationships.

Susan stated that she has a strong desire to have children and to have a Christian marriage; however, as she faces her thirty-ninth birthday she is recognizing that this is not likely. She is frustrated by well-meaning efforts of others to find a man for her, and sometimes she is angry with God for withholding motherhood from her. She says that now she is looking to find meaning and fulfillment in the life God has given her and to come to terms with "being single in a married world," although she is still ambivalent about this goal. Susan states that she is looking to find peace in her circumstances and to find meaning in her occupational/vocational life. While she is open to exploring other career and work options that might be more meaningful, she needs to have a certain monetary income in order to meet legitimate financial obligations she has incurred over the years both on her own and in helping family members.

## Discussion Questions

1. How did you feel as you read Susan's case? Did you feel a sense of sadness? Did you feel hope? Counselees often arouse feelings in their counselors, and these feelings, in turn, can influ-

ence the counseling. How might your feelings about Susan's case influence you?

2. Why do you think Susan still is single? In what ways might your answer to this question impact your counseling work with Susan?

3. The *Christian Counseling* book talks about the effects of singleness. Which of these do you see in Susan? How might these be impacting her life? How would you help Susan deal with each of these?

4. Susan's goals for counseling appear to be vague. How would you help her focus on some goals for her life and move forward?

5. Remember the presenting problem, that Susan felt confused and overwhelmed by life. How would you help her with these issues? How would you help her "find peace in her circumstances" and "find meaning in her occupational/vocational life"?

6. What approaches will you take in counseling Susan? Give reasons for your answer.

7. In what ways are Susan's family members helping and hindering her in the search to find meaning and fulfillment in her life? Answer the same question about Susan's church. What about Susan's work? What about her friends, including the other women at work and the friends who keep trying to find a man for Susan? How will your answers to these questions impact the way you counsel Susan?

8. Susan is open to exploring other career and work options. Give reasons why this would be a good approach to helping Susan. What reasons do you have for not taking this approach but, instead, encouraging Susan to keep her present job while she focuses on other things?

## General Questions

1. Would it make any difference who counseled Susan? Would she be better served by seeing a single person or one who is married, a man or a woman, somebody younger than her or somebody older? Give reasons for your answers.

2. How could you help a church be more sensitive to singles than the church that Susan attends where the women's ministry is focused on young moms?

3. As a counselor, how could you help Susan and people like her to avoid and prevent the common problems of singleness that are outlined in the *Christian Counseling* book?

### Personal Reflection Questions

1. Like Susan, do you feel confused and overwhelmed by life? If so, in what ways will this influence your counseling with people like Susan? Write your answers in a journal and consider discussing this with somebody you trust.

2. If you are single, what feelings have this chapter and the parallel chapter in *Christian Counseling* aroused in you? In what ways are you like Susan? In what ways are you different? If you have struggles with singleness like Susan has, are you qualified to counsel single people? Give reasons for your answer.

3. If you are married, how do you respond to Susan's struggles? Do they have relevance to your own life and counseling work?

For a follow-up to the story of Susan, please go to the Epilogue at the end of the book.

# 27

## Choosing a Marriage Partner

Why do people want to get married but remain single? There can be many reasons, of course, but sometimes a person's background, fears, and self-defeating behaviors get in the way of progress toward marriage. This is true of Jeff, who appears to have sabotaged several relationships that may have led to marriage. His story illustrates the significant role that counseling may play in helping people get past the obstacles that can prevent them from finding and committing to a marriage partner.

Jeff is thirty-three and still single. He very much wants to get married, but he hasn't found a marriage partner, so he has come to discuss this with a counselor.

Jeff grew up as the middle child in a home where both the father and the mother were verbally and physically abusive. Both parents were heavily involved with their careers, often gone from home, and minimally involved with their children, even when they were little. Before he was ten, Jeff's parents divorced, and he and his other siblings lived with their mother. Jeff never saw reciprocating healthy love in his home, and he never had a model of a good marriage. He dated some when he was in high school and college, but he kept so busy with school, work, campus ministry leadership, sports, and friends that there was not much time for dating. Whenever he did date, Jeff typically would start a relationship with passion and romance that would last for a couple of months and then fade. He explained that he enjoyed these women very much, but after a few weeks he would feel that the relationship was not going any further, so he would break it up.

When he was about age twenty-two, Jeff was dating a woman and came to the point where he would typically end the relationship, but this time he did not want to do so. He told her that he felt like the relationship needed to end or take a step forward, but he didn't know what that step forward looked like. Her response stunned him. "Jeff," she said, "I love you." He was so shocked by her words that he walked away speechless. Two days later they talked again, and he too said the words "I love you." He describes this as the day and the relationship in which he first learned to love. This woman was very attractive and highly intelligent. Jeff was terrified of losing her love. He also was concerned because she tended to be depressed, was suicidal at times, and had struggled with bulimia. For over a year theirs was a dramatic push-and-pull relationship that spiraled downward: as she drew him close, he tried to save her; she would push him away, and he would try to pull her closer but meet greater resistance. After they went their separate ways, Jeff came to recognize that he had been protecting himself from love and closeness by being with someone who would keep pushing him away. He vowed that he would never again enter into a similar unhealthy relationship.

Then it happened again. Jeff found himself in love with a dynamic woman who would draw him in, become afraid, and then push him away. He moved to another city to be with her, and once again he became terrified lest he lose her love. He would try to pull her closer and force the relationship to work. In response to this she became claustrophobic and eventually broke up with him. Later, after Jeff had moved back to his home state, the woman wanted to restart the relationship, and they tried to make it work even though they were distant from one another. A year or two later, Jeff dated a different woman for about eight months hoping it would turn to love. He broke up with her when it didn't happen.

The cycle began again after Jeff turned thirty. He began a passionate long-distance relationship with a woman named Lisa who seemed to pursue him consistently without pulling away in fear. Several months later he took a new job and moved to the city where she was living so they could be closer. When he saw that the relationship was heading toward marriage, Jeff became fearful that he might be making the wrong decision. To prevent this, he became extremely critical of this woman who loved him. He hated what was happening but felt unable to escape the patterns that he had developed. Lisa withdrew from the relationship so that both could have space and time to re-evaluate where they were.

It was at this point that Jeff started seeing a counselor. He wants to deal with the ongoing fears and to learn how to break the cycle that is keeping him from marriage. He wonders if part of his problem comes from the violence and the lack of love in the home where he grew up. He still wants very much to get married, to experience the healthy marriage that he never saw at home. How can Jeff be helped?

## Discussion Questions

1. Jeff is a successful, intelligent, attractive, socially adept young professional who is a skilled athlete and a committed Christian. Look over his life story again and review what you know about the reasons why some people do not get married. List the reasons why Jeff is still single.
2. With this list in mind, what would be your approach in counseling Jeff?
3. What would be your goals? Notice Jeff's goals listed in the last paragraph of his story. Which goals would you start working on first? Give reasons for your answer.
4. Describe the cycle of behavior that appears to have trapped Jeff. How would you help him break this?
5. What are Jeff's fears? How can he be helped to be less fearful?
6. In what practical ways will you bring a Christian perspective into Jeff's counseling?
7. At this point would you bring Lisa into the counseling relationship? Give reasons both for and against Lisa's involvement.

## General Questions

1. Why is there hope that Jeff will get married within the next five years? Give reasons for your answer. Why might you share

these reasons with Jeff? In contrast, what is the evidence that Jeff will be unsuccessful in choosing a mate and committing to marriage?

2.  Discuss the role of Jeff's family background as it relates to his desire for marriage. In what ways might Lisa's background influence the relationship?

3.  Given what you know about Jeff's background, what problems might come up in a future marriage? How could you help Jeff anticipate and prevent these problems? Be specific.

4.  To move toward marriage, Jeff needs to deal with some background issues. How would you check to see if there are other background, personality, attitude, or other relationship issues that you don't know about but that could be sabotaging Jeff's search for a mate?

5.  Make a prediction. Do you think Jeff and Lisa will go back to rebuilding their relationship and move toward marriage? Give reasons for your answer. The *Christian Counseling* book lists reasons why some people choose wisely in their mate selection. How many of these apply to Jeff and Lisa?

### Personal Reflection Questions

1.  Are you married? If not, what might be reasons for your singleness? In answering, draw on what you have learned from Jeff and from reading chapter 27 in the *Christian Counseling* book.

2.  If you are single, what are the obstacles to marriage in your life? How will you deal with these? Be specific. Who will help you deal with these?

3.  Answer question 1 again, but apply your answer to some friend or other single person that you know.

4.  If you are married, what has your study of this topic revealed about issues in your life that could adversely or positively impact your marriage?

5.  Jeff benefited from talking to a counselor as he dealt with the issues and attitudes in his life that would impact marriage. What are the reasons why you, too, could benefit from counseling on issues like these? What are the reasons why you

should not go for this kind of counseling? If you do decide to seek a counselor, to whom would you go for counseling? When will you go? What might hold you back from going?

For a follow-up to the story of Jeff, please go to the Epilogue at the end of the book.

## PART SIX

# Family Issues

# 28

# Premarital Counseling

In the middle of a sermon on marriage, a pastor made this statement about premarital counseling: "It rarely works. By the time a couple gets to the counselor, they already have made up their minds about getting married and they aren't much interested in anything apart from each other or the plans for their wedding." The following story about Leslie and Tony might challenge the pastor's somewhat pessimistic assessment of premarital counseling.

Leslie and Tony, ages twenty-two and twenty-one, respectively, met at a church youth group four years before they appeared for premarital counseling. They both came from church backgrounds and were quick to point out that in addition to being an engaged couple, they were the best of friends.

Tony is the oldest child in a family of four boys. His mother is mentally disabled, probably with a borderline personality disorder. Tony's father is an alcoholic who works in a blue-collar industry where he has had a troubled work history. When Tony was ten, the parents divorced and Tony went to live with his mother. Because of growing tension and conflict between the mother and Tony, he moved when he was fifteen and went to live with the father and his new wife. Despite this troubled family history, Tony has felt the love of his parents and has a positive relationship with each of them.

Leslie's family history has been more stable than that of her fiancé. She describes her parents as being easygoing, caring, and responsible.

The father has held a steady job at the same company for many years, and the mother has been a homemaker. They have been married for more than twenty-five years and have a home where there are warm relationships and little conflict but also little physical affection. Leslie knows of her parents' love because of their verbal affirmations over the years and their consistent loving actions toward their children. Perhaps because of this stable family background, Leslie appears to be blind to her fiancé's family history and to the impact that this might have on the marriage.

The couple gives evidence of being very responsible, committed to each other, without a history of major conflict, and with a strong Christian faith. Tony has completed two years of college and has every intention of continuing until he gets his degree, after which he would like to go to graduate school. He appears to be highly ambitious but also shows a tendency to impulsivity. Leslie has completed her degree in Christian education with an emphasis on children. She would like to teach and also attend graduate school some day, but after their marriage Leslie plans to work to support the family while Tony finishes his education. Following their wedding, Leslie and Tony plan to move away from the area where they grew up so they can continue with their educational plans. Both want children but not until their educations are completed and their careers are established. Neither has been sexually active, and they both display a naiveté concerning sexuality.

## Discussion Questions

1. What are indications that Leslie and Tony will have a successful marriage? What might create problems for their marriage?
2. Based on your answers to the previous questions, in what ways do you think Leslie and Tony could benefit from premarital counseling?
3. What would be some of your goals in working with them?
4. In what ways will their family backgrounds impact their marriage? How will you deal with this in your counseling?
5. In what ways will their sexual naiveté impact their marriage? How will you deal with this in premarital counseling?
6. What evidence do you see, if any, that they should not get

married at this point in their lives? What is the evidence that a marriage for them would be a wise decision?

## General Questions

1. In premarital counseling, does it matter if the counselor is married? Give reasons for your answer. What are the advantages and disadvantages of having a married counselor? What are advantages and disadvantages of having a premarital counselor who is single?
2. For Tony and Leslie, what are the advantages and disadvantages of their plans to move away from where they grew up?
3. What are the advantages and disadvantages of their plans to have Leslie work to support her new husband? How realistic is their planning? How will you raise this in your counseling? To what extent, if any, will your premarital counseling include a discussion of financial issues?
4. As a counselor, what can you do to prevent unhealthy marriages in couples who are engaged but still single?
5. Read the pastor's comment in the first paragraph of this chapter. Do you agree? Give reasons for your answer.

## Personal Reflection Questions

1. What discomforts, if any, do you have about discussing sex with this couple? How specific will you be? How will you deal with your own discomforts in discussing their sexual relationship? Jot down your answers in a journal. You may want to discuss this with a counselor or trusted friend.
2. Assume that a couple comes for premarital counseling but you sense that the marriage will not be healthy. How will you dissuade them from getting married? How do you feel about this kind of unpopular intervention in the lives of counselees? What could you do to improve in this kind of counseling?

For a follow-up to the story of Tony and Leslie, please go to the Epilogue at the end of the book.

# 29

# Marriage Issues

Marriage counseling from a distinctly Christian perspective is often filled with intense challenges. Perhaps it would be less so if separation were a more acceptable option or if God would routinely deliver his followers from both their backgrounds and themselves. Consider the struggle of Jack and Jill who have what their counselor calls "a stuck-in-the-mud marriage."

When they came to the office, this couple was beginning their third attempt at Christian marriage counseling, and they both agreed that it would be the last. The first counselor routinely forgot critical information about their story from week to week. The second counselor fell asleep. Expectations were low this third time around, but the stakes were extremely high. Jack and Jill are both on the worship team of their charismatic church. A traveling prophetic minister, who knew nothing about them, had prayed over them and told them that he could see "mud" all over the place. He said that the enemy had been throwing mud at them and that they were in the midst of a raging spiritual battle that had the intensity of a fiery furnace. This prophet gave encouragement because he saw a bright future but did say that there was much heat yet to endure. It was the hope of the bright future that prompted a last attempt to salvage this relationship that was deeply distressed.

Jack and Jill are forty-one and thirty-one years old, respectively, and have been married for five years, although they have been in this relationship for a total of twelve years. There are no children, and this adds a subtle pressure to the urgency to get the marriage right because both sense the "clock" ticking. When they describe their marriage, it does not take long for them to get to the muddy side of the relationship. "We have difficulty resolving conflict" is how the story begins. There have been anger and domestic-violence issues since the beginning of the relationship. Conflicts occur daily. The heat increases in an escalating pattern of at least weekly ugly verbal arguments. As the fire burns, the battle gets physical about once a month. Both own some responsibility for this. Jack actually loses awareness of what he's doing and doesn't remember it later. The violence includes open-handed hitting, grabbing, shaking with vice-like grip, charging, screaming, and breaking things. Jill is devastated by Jack's anger and outbursts. Even so, she admits that she holds on to every wrong thing he has ever done, and she tosses these memories at him whenever the mud starts to fly. He often pleads with Jill to leave him alone when he can tell he is going to have an outburst, but she will not and frequently goads him into an outburst. They report that nearly all the worst of these episodes occur after 9:00 p.m. A sign of hope is that the new counselor hears a clear admission of each person's contributions to the problem. There is grief, remorse, and ready tearfulness, yet a sense of desperation as if the mud of their conflict has now been baked into the clay of their destiny.

Jill's family has insisted that she press charges and leave Jack. As a family, they have shamed and ostracized her while refusing to have any contact with her husband. Both of their families are Christian. Jack and Jill do not believe in divorce. They want to have children but would not think of bringing a child into a relationship like they have now. They are intelligent, outwardly successful, and highly motivated. They come requesting help to save their marriage. They want to make the changes necessary in order to resolve conflict safely, repair trust, and gain enough confidence to begin making plans for a family.

Jack admits to "workaholism." He recognizes that this driven activity shows his need for a sense of self-worth that he is seeking at work, church, and home. He reports feeling constantly resentful of how much he has to do while always feeling under-appreciated. There are signs of depression with a self-confessed terror of emotional intimacy. He wants sexual relations more regularly but admits to constantly disappointing Jill romantically. Jack's father was an alcoholic who would yell and hit the mother when he got drunk. Jack is aware that he is a victim of emotional neglect and verbal cruelty by his father. His only memories of his father are of critical remarks. It was impossible to get his father's attention at home, so Jack poured himself into school, where he was rewarded for being helpful and a hard worker. The pattern persists.

Jill is ready to call herself a "perfectionist." She sees this in how she handles her managerial position at work, in her home, and in her person. Her biggest fear is that of being left alone. Thus, she admits to both attention-seeking and people-pleasing behavior. Her mother is also an alcoholic, and Jill has pushed hard during her entire life to please her mother and gain approval. Although Jill does not see much further into her own personality trends, the counselor hears much evidence of poor boundaries in her relationships, patterns of enmeshment, enabling, and pushing stressful emotions into physical pains and discomforts. In her upbringing Jill was rewarded in her family by keeping silent, looking good, and being a peacemaker. Somehow these patterns are not working too well with Jack, and their muddied marriage is near the point of being burned up.

## Discussion Questions

1. As the counselor for this couple, you already know the importance of remembering details from week to week and of not falling asleep in counseling sessions. As they now sit in your presence, what are the first things you will say or do to help them?

2. The *Christian Counseling* book discusses issues that undermine marriages. Which of these issues might be undermining the marriage of Jack and Jill? In counseling, how might these undermining influences be stopped?

3. What behaviors and attitudes—both in Jack and in Jill—are keeping this marriage from getting better?

4. What are the signs that the marriage has hope? How would these hopeful signs be useful in your marriage counseling?

5. In the introduction to this case, the counselor implied that Jack and Jill's problems may arise from their backgrounds. What

background issues are making their marriage worse? How can these issues be prevented from continuing to exert an influence?

6. In what ways did the visiting preacher's prayer and vision hinder and/or help this couple? In your counseling would you discuss this prayer with the couple? What would be your purpose in doing so?

7. In counseling with this couple, what goals would you have? What would be good reasons for discussing goals with both Jack and Jill?

8. What are process issues (see the *Christian Counseling* book), and how might these be applied to Jack and Jill's relationship?

## General Questions

1. There is abuse in this relationship. Would you report this to authorities? What would be your reasons for doing this? How would this impact your work with them as a counselor?

2. Would you insist on participation in a domestic-violence group program as part of Jack and Jill's counseling? Give reasons for either insisting that there be participation in such a program and reasons for not making that recommendation.

3. How might systems theory explain Jack and Jill's relationship?

4. How might systems theory help with your counseling?

5. What are the biblical grounds for divorce that might apply to this couple?

6. Should Jack and Jill step down from their ministry in the church? Give reasons for your answer.

7. What reading might you recommend for this couple? Would reading help? Give reasons for your answer.

## Personal Reflection Questions

1. Read the following questions adapted from the *Christian Counseling* book:
   - What is your attitude toward marital problems?
   - Are you critical of those who have marital difficulties? Are you inclined to condemn, prone to take sides, annoyed

because these problems take so much time from your schedule, afraid that marital counseling might arouse anxieties about your own marriage? Give examples to support your answers.

- What prejudices might you have about marriage that could interfere with your objectivity—views such as the conviction that men need to be dominant or that women should give up their careers to care for their families?
- What specific issues make you nervous about working as a marriage counselor?
- Answer these questions on paper and/or in discussion with some person that you trust.

2. *Christian Counseling* discusses common mistakes that marriage counselors make. Which of these might be most likely to appear in your counseling? What can you do now to avoid these mistakes later?

For a follow-up to the story of Jack and Jill, please go to the Epilogue at the end of the book.

# 30

# Pregnancy Issues

Every day probably thousands of couples and single women are shocked to discover that an unwanted pregnancy has occurred. In equal numbers, perhaps, other thousands discover that another month has passed with no baby being conceived. Both of these can create disappointment and a host of other emotions in the people whose lives are being impacted by unwanted or unexpected pregnancies or by continual reminders of infertility.

Tim and Cindy had been married for thirteen years when she came to the counselor's office. During their courtship they dreamed about their life together, and in the center of that dream was the thought of having children. At first they took precautions to prevent an early pregnancy, but when they were ready to start their family Cindy didn't get pregnant. For two years they tried to conceive. Twice a pregnancy got started, but they lost each baby within the first few weeks and plunged back into deep disappointment and efforts to try again. Their lack of success eventually led them to see a specialist who tested them both—sometimes with embarrassing procedures—and gave them instructions on ways to conceive.

For almost ten years Tim and Cindy have met with a variety of infertility specialists, cooperated in trying a variety of options for getting pregnant, and agreed to some very invasive medical procedures. Every month they would wait to see if a pregnancy had occurred.

Every month they were disappointed. Tens of thousands of dollars and many frustrations later they still had no children. Eventually it was found that Cindy's reproductive system was not functioning properly, explaining why the full-term pregnancy that they so much wanted had never occurred.

About a year prior to their counseling appointment, the couple had faced a major decision. One of the women at their church, a long-time friend of Cindy's, offered to be a surrogate mother. She suggested that Tim's sperm could be collected and used in the laboratory to fertilize eggs taken from Cindy's uterus and then implanted in the friend's body. She would carry the baby to full term as a surrogate mother. It was an unexpected and unsettling offer. It also was a procedure that might work and give them a baby of their own. Since the fertilized egg would be implanted in the other woman, the total genetic makeup of the baby would come from the couple. Tim and Cindy discussed this with some close friends, talked with a pastor and their doctor, and spent hours looking at surrogate pregnancy and IVF (in vitro fertilization) materials on the Internet. Despite the encouragement of some Christian friends, the couple wondered about the ethics of such a decision. They met with a couple who had two IVF children, debated about the alternative of using a surrogate mother that they did not know, and pondered whether there would be unanticipated long-term obligations or relationship problems that might arise if the friend did carry their baby.

Well aware that they were both getting older, they nevertheless decided to turn down the offer of their friend, at least temporarily, and explore the option of adopting a child. As a requirement for this process the adoption agency referred Cindy for counseling. At the beginning she admitted that she had been annoyed at the thought of having to see a psychologist. She was "afraid of being psychoanalyzed" and was fearful that she might say the wrong things and jeopardize her ability to become a mother. She became visibly more relaxed after the counselor gave a brief explanation of what would be involved and gave Cindy the opportunity to state her own treatment goals.

Cindy indicated that she and Tim were still very much in love, but both realized that their relationship had suffered under the weight of their infertility. Cindy admitted that she had become emotionally numb to the disappointments of failed attempts to get pregnant. Four years earlier she had lost hope of conceiving but continued with the "poking and prodding" of specialists because she did not want to disappoint her husband. This seemed to be an adaptive attempt to shield herself from the monthly letdowns that she had come to believe were inevitable. However, it was taking a secret toll on her personality as well as on her marriage. Ridden with guilt and anger, she knew that she was becoming emotionally distant.

## Discussion Questions

1. When she came for counseling, Cindy "became visibly more relaxed after the counselor gave a brief explanation of what would be involved." Assume that you had been the counselor. What explanation would you have given to Cindy about what would be involved in the counseling?

2. What might be the reasons for Cindy's guilt, anger, and emotional distance from her husband? How would you counsel Cindy concerning each of these issues?

3. The adoption agency referred Cindy for counseling. What would be your reasons for and against having Tim involved in the counseling as well? Would you counsel them separately or together? Give reasons for each alternative.

4. How would you bring a Christian perspective into your counseling? How, if at all, would you use the Scriptures in counseling this couple? How might stories such as those of Sarah, Rachel, Hannah, or Elizabeth (the wife of Zechariah) bring comfort or discouragement to Tim and Cindy?

5. Suppose that Cindy is angry with God because he has not allowed them to have children. How would you help Cindy and Tim deal with this anger?

6. Imagine that Tim and Cindy have friends or relatives who have had no problems with infertility and who have healthy children. Tim and Cindy feel especially sad and uncomfortable in the presence of these friends and their children. The friends, in turn, feel uncomfortable inviting Tim and Cindy to social gath-

erings because these remind the couple of their infertility. How would you help these people deal with their discomforts and awkward feelings?

## General Questions

1. Based on what you know about Cindy and Tim, why do you think the adoption agency wanted Cindy to come for counseling before they agreed to move forward with the adoption? If Cindy gave her permission for you to talk with the person who referred her, what information would you want to know? What difference would this make in your counseling?

2. Assume that Cindy and Tim came together and wanted counseling about whether or not they should move forward with IVF and the services of a surrogate mother? How would you counsel them?

3. What follows are quotations taken from a Christian posting on the Internet. Do you agree or disagree with each of these statements? Give reasons for your answers.

   - It would not be acceptable for a woman to carry another couple's child if that woman were to have sexual relations with the man who is not her husband in order to become impregnated. This would be adultery.
   - Nor would it be acceptable for a man whose wife could not conceive to have sexual relations with a surrogate mother, who is not his wife. This would be adultery.
   - Surrogate motherhood is permissible if there is no sexual intercourse and if the seed of the man does not enter the womb of a woman to whom he is not married, except via an already fertilized egg.

## Personal Reflection Questions

1. Think of a person or couple you know that has had pregnancy-related problems—unwanted pregnancies, inability to get or retain a pregnancy, or a perinatal loss. If possible, think of someone specific. If you have had a pregnancy-related problem in your own life, then think about yourself.

- How did this issue impact the person(s) you have in mind both short-term and in the long run?
- In what ways will this impact how you counsel people with pregnancy-related problems? Be specific.

For a follow-up to the story or Cindy and Tim, please go to the Epilogue at the end of the book.

# 31

# Family Issues

This book gives almost fifty stories of people who have had problems that were brought to counselors. In almost every one of these life stories a family has been impacted or involved in some way. In many ways, therefore, this is a book about family issues. With Pastor R, however, the major focus of the problem involves both his church family and his family at home.

Pastor R is in his mid-thirties, married to Tracy, father of three children, and assistant pastor of a respected church in a mid-sized city. Pastor R grew up in a Christian home, the son of a pastor and his wife who led a small church in a rural area. Both parents taught and modeled the importance of helping and serving others.

After seminary, Pastor R and Tracy moved to their current home, next to the church building. Pastor R is a friendly person who is popular among church members, many of whom are in the habit of dropping by the assistant pastor's home, without prior warning, to say hello and sometimes to talk. Everybody agrees that their assistant pastor is a good listener. If he is not at home when the unannounced visitors arrive, they feel free to stay for a while and talk to his wife and children.

The senior pastor of the church is much older than Pastor R. Although the two men don't feel a special closeness to each other, they get along fine and without any conflict. In fact, they each go about their own work and hardly see each other apart from church services or the elder meetings. When they do get together, the senior pastor likes to talk—brag might be a better word—about his vision for the church and about how God has used him to be the founder and builder of the ministry. Recently he talked to Pastor R about a new program that needed to be started and asked the younger man if he could take responsibility for getting it going. Pastor R's main ministry is visiting families, especially those who are in crisis, suffering from loss, or facing family problems. Additionally, he is responsible for overseeing all the small groups in the church, a ministry that was started two years earlier and has been growing since then.

Pastor R is overwhelmed with his work. It seems that there is not enough time in his day to visit families, take care of his administrative responsibilities, deal with the personal and pastoral care needs of the congregation, prepare to teach an adult Bible class on Sundays, and spend time with God. For the first several years at this church, Pastor R took Saturdays off, but not anymore. He works seven days a week and recently has begun to visit families on Saturdays when they are home from work.

When he returned home one evening recently, Pastor R's three-year-old daughter ran to the door to welcome him and tell him about her day. This has been her regular routine for some time. As the little girl talked enthusiastically and her father tried to put other things out of his mind and listen, the cell phone rang. He pulled it from his pocket and impatiently moved it around in his hand. Maybe a family in the church needed his help. However, something stopped him from answering this time. It was his daughter's little voice. "Daddy," she said somewhat plaintively, "you used to look at me when I talked to you. Then you would say 'You are so pretty.'" She stopped for a few seconds and then she added, "You don't do that anymore."

If you could ask him, Pastor R would admit that he has not been giving much attention to his family lately. His wife is getting weary from the steady stream of visitors and the incessant demands of three young children. The couple rarely spends time together, and in many ways they have been going their separate ways even though they live in the same house and sleep in the same bed. Pastor R feels guilty about this neglect of his marriage and his family, but he also feels guilty if he is not available to respond to the needs of the people in his congregation and community. Whenever his wife suggests that they go on a vacation and that Pastor R needs to spend more time with his family, he responds that he would love to do this but as a minister he believes that God must come first in his life. He reminds Tracy about the impact that they are having and about what they are doing in people's lives. He tells her that there will be more time in the future and that some day they can have a nice vacation.

In the meantime, Pastor R keeps getting busier, the visitors keep dropping by, the family is less and less together, and Tracy gets more frustrated. In the middle of all this, the pressured man who genuinely cares so much about other people is considering the offer to take on another church project. In his heart he knows that this is one more responsibility that can further divide his family, weaken his marriage, and increase everybody's stress.

## Discussion Questions

1. Assume that you are a counselor in Pastor R's congregation. From a distance you can see what is happening to his family so you invite the young pastor to lunch, where you plan to challenge him to slow down and to get some counseling. How would you approach him over lunch in a way that would help him see his need and be open to the possibility of getting counseling help?

2. From what you can observe, what is creating the problems in Pastor R's family?

3. Assuming that the pastor and Tracy would be open to counseling, how could the emerging family problems be stopped from getting worse and their relationship with each other and their children be improved?

4. If you were a counselor working with Pastor R and his family, what would be your counseling goals? What methods would you use?

5. In what ways is the church contributing to this family's problems? What needs to change? How could this be done?

6. What attitudes and behaviors in Pastor R are contributing to the escalating problems in their family?

7. Where is God in this family and this church? How would you bring God and your Christian perspectives into counseling Pastor R and Tracy?

### General Questions

1. Give reasons for and against involving the senior pastor and the church elders in helping this pastor and his family deal with their growing problems.

2. The two pastors obviously work independently and do not function as a team. How does this contribute to Pastor R's problems? What can and should be done about this working relationship? In what ways could changes help Pastor R and his family?

3. The *Christian Counseling* book describes the Levels of Family Involvement (LFI) model that originated with psychologist William J. Doherty. What are these five levels, and where would you intervene if you were counseling Pastor R and his family?

4. What resources does this family have that can enable it to fend off a family crisis and grow into a healthier family?

### Personal Reflection Questions

1. This consideration of family issues is a good opportunity to look at our own families and their influence, whether or not we are married. In what ways has your family background influenced the way you are now? How does this or will this impact your counseling?

2. Think of your current family situation. Where do your relationships with your family need attention and improvement? What needs to be done, specifically? Write your answers in a secure place. When will you take needed action? What are the benefits of having somebody who will hold you accountable? Who is that person?

3. In what ways, if any, are you like Pastor R, who is overly involved with his work and neglectful of his family? How will you change? Be specific.

4. How will your current family situation influence the way you counsel, especially the ways in which you counsel families?

For a follow-up to the story of Pastor R, please go to the Epilogue at the end of the book.

# 32

# Divorce and Remarriage

The issues of divorce and remarriage have long been debated. Although the Bible gives clear answers on this issue, each couple that comes for counseling seems to bring specifics that do not always fit neatly into the scenarios offered in Scripture. Peter and Mary are an example.

Peter is a forty-year-old white male who has been married for nineteen years. He lives with his wife (Mary) and three children. The oldest child is a twenty-two-year-old male that Peter calls his own, although he is not the biological father. The son was born to Peter's wife prior to their relationship. Jill is their teenage daughter, and Billy is their nine-year-old son. This family rents a small three-bedroom home in the suburbs where Peter is employed as a manager for a company that repairs copy machines. Peter grew up attending an evangelical church and participated very actively in a parachurch children's ministry during his elementary school years. When he reached the teenage years, however, Peter drifted away from the church. He became very promiscuous and frequently was involved with alcohol, drugs, and gambling. As a teenager he once was in a drug rehabilitation program but describes his experiences there as being of no value because the other participants saw him as a kid who did not need to be taken seriously or given the help he needed. Years later, when he came for counseling, Peter had been free of his addictions for about eighteen months as the result of a twelve-step recovery program.

Although he described himself as a Christian, Peter stated that he felt far from God. He had not attended church for many years but had started going again when his youngest children got involved with the church youth group. He now attends church regularly, most often without his wife. She does not have a religious background and works part time as a cashier at a local supermarket, so she is usually at work on Sundays. Like her husband, Mary also used drugs and alcohol earlier in their marriage. She has had two bouts of cancer but has been cancer-free for fifteen months.

Peter asked for counseling to discuss his marital difficulties. Specifically, he wanted to talk with a pastoral counselor in hopes of getting pastoral approval for a divorce. Peter describes his nineteen-year marriage as never having a season of happiness. The couple dated for five months before their marriage ceremony, which was prompted by Mary's pregnancy with their first child. Peter has been in therapy on two separate occasions to deal with depression and addiction issues. Four years ago he separated from his wife for a period of three months but returned home for the sake of his children and because his wife promised to get help for her own depression.

After the counselor had met with Peter for a few sessions, Mary came for counseling along with her husband. The couple agreed that their sexual intimacy is the best part of their marriage although both have had extramarital affairs and have included third parties into their sexual relationship. The affairs committed by his wife were encouraged by Peter, who suggested that extramarital sex would enhance their own sexual intimacy. The last affair ended over twelve months ago.

Mary wants to stay in the marriage and would like to have marital counseling, but Peter is less enthusiastic about this idea. He describes himself as being tired and states that he does not have the energy to stick with this marriage that has never brought him any happiness. Mary has begun meeting with another counselor, but Peter wants to stay with the present counselor to work on a variety of issues, but especially to get direction regarding his desire to divorce.

### Discussion Questions

1. What does the Bible say about Peter and Mary's situation? Based on biblical teachings, are they free to divorce?

2.  What is there about Peter and Mary's situation that does not appear to be addressed in Scripture?
3.  Assume that you are Peter's counselor. He has made another appointment and wants to know if it is OK for him to file for divorce. What are you going to do or say when he arrives? What are the reasons for doing what you plan to do?
4.  Will you give your approval for the divorce? Why or why not? Assume that Peter is pressing you for an answer.
5.  Assume that you will continue to work with Peter. What will be your goals for counseling whether or not they get a divorce?
6.  Assume that Peter and Mary stay together. How will this impact their relationship, their children, their quality of life, and their relationships with God?
7.  Assume that Peter and Mary decide to get a divorce, regardless of your counseling. How will the divorce impact their relationship, their children, their quality of life, and their relationships with God?
8.  From a biblical perspective, would Peter and Mary be free to enter into new marriages if they get a divorce?

## General Questions

1.  Peter and Mary are being seen by different counselors. How would you work in partnership with Mary's counselor, without violating any ethical principles? What are the reasons in favor of this couple being seen together? What are the reasons to support their staying with separate counselors? Are there other alternatives?
2.  What are the issues in Peter's life that have contributed to his desire to get a divorce? How could these have been prevented or dealt with earlier in Peter's life?
3.  Peter has found satisfaction serving in the church. Are there biblical or other reasons why he should not be serving in the church? What are the reasons why it is acceptable for him to serve? How will you answer these questions differently if he and Mary get a divorce?
4.  Assuming that Peter and Mary get a divorce, how would you help Peter rebuild his life?

5.  How would you help Peter rebuild his life if the couple does not get divorced?

## Personal Reflection Questions

1.  Be honest with yourself and perhaps with a trusted friend as you answer the following questions. You may want to ponder these questions before God and seek his guidance. Then express your answers in a journal.

    - Apart from what you might say to Peter, do you think divorce is acceptable for him? Is it wise? Are there similar cases that you know about where issues like these have arisen?
    - If Peter gets a divorce, is he free to remarry? What about Mary?
    - Assume that Peter is your father or your brother. Would your answers to any of the above questions be different? (Sometimes it is easy to give answers in abstract or impersonal situations, but the answers are harder when a situation like this arises in our own families.)

2.  As a counselor, how will you feel when somebody like Peter or Mary arrives in your office? What biases might influence your counseling? What biblical principles will guide your work?

3.  How could the case of Peter and Mary be relevant to your own marriage or to a marriage in your own family? How would you or your marriage be impacted by counseling with Peter and/or Mary? What can you learn from their example? Be specific.

4.  What are reasons why you should not deal with cases like these? (Perhaps all counselors have some problem areas that they should avoid.) If you don't see people like this, what might this say about you, positively or negatively?

For a follow-up to the story of Peter and Mary, please go to the Epilogue at the end of the book.

PART SEVEN

# Control Issues

# 33

# Mental Disorders

Mental disorders take many forms. Sometimes abnormal thinking or behavior is barely noticeable. In other cases the disorder is highly visible. In the man whose story follows, life appeared to be relatively normal. He was able to live alone and take care of himself with competence. He had a business and regularly attended church, but he also showed behavior that was highly unusual.

Mr. D is in his mid-thirties, divorced, lonely, and struggling to build a small landscaping business. He grew up as an only child in a family where he felt ignored. His father was consumed with work and rarely home. The mother had a schizophrenic disorder and often "seemed to be in her own little world." As a young man Mr. D found some acceptance at a neighborhood church, and it was there that he hoped to someday find a wife who would give him the support and companionship that he craved. One night as he prayed, Mr. D heard a voice telling him that he soon would get married to a woman named Beverly. When he met somebody with that name a few days later, Mr. D concluded that this was his future wife. The couple had a whirlwind courtship and got married four weeks after their first meeting.

The marriage was not easy, and the couple had divorced shortly before Mr. D came for his first counseling appointment. He entered the room supported by a cane and explained that he had a progressive muscular disorder that limited his mobility and interfered with his ability to walk and to work. It soon became clear that this man also had difficulties with interpersonal relationships. Whenever there was even a hint of criticism from customers, vendors, or others, Mr. D would misinterpret what was being said, respond with hostility, and explode with anger. He realized that these outbursts were hurting his business, but even so, he talked often about expanding and spent a large amount of money on new equipment that was not needed and rarely used.

As he described these new tools in one of the sessions, the counselee asked if the counselor ever heard voices. Before waiting for an answer, Mr. D said that he had heard a voice that morning, telling him to use one of the new tools to kill the counselor. Calmly, the counselor asked for more details about what the voice had said, and eventually Mr. D agreed that killing his counselor was not a wise decision.

Shortly thereafter, Mr. D said that he was building a small network of people who could be available to help in an emergency, should he ever fall because of his physical disability. The counselor, who was also a pastor, reluctantly agreed to be on this helping team, and one night a distressed call came from Mr. D. He said that he had fallen. He was on the floor and could not get up, but he had called the paramedics and wanted somebody to come from the church. Mindful of his own need for protection, the counselor picked up a friend, and together they went to Mr. D's home, arriving at about the same time as the police and an ambulance. In vivid detail, Mr. D told how he had been attacked and knocked to the floor by vandals who had broken into his visibly disheveled apartment. Independently, both the counselor and the police had doubts about the accuracy of the story, and after a lot of questioning, Mr. D admitted that he had made up the story and faked the home invasion. A few weeks thereafter it was determined that the reported physical disability was also a deception.

### Discussion Questions

1.  Assume that you are Mr. D's counselor. He claims that your counseling is helpful and he is coming soon for an appointment following the preceding episode. What will you do?
2.  The introduction of this case describes Mr. D as a man who "appeared to be relatively normal. He was able to live alone and take care of himself with competence. He had a business

and regularly attended church." What is the evidence that Mr. D has a mental disorder? What is the evidence that he does not have a mental disorder?

3. Look over Table 33–1 in *Christian Counseling*. Where might Mr. D fit?

4. Assume that you are Mr. D's counselor. List the questions that would help you understand and help him better. What are your reasons for seeking answers to each of these questions?

5. *Christian Counseling* lists some causes of mental disorders. Which of these, if any, apply in the case of Mr. D?

6. Would you continue to counsel Mr. D? Give reasons for your answer. If you are discussing this case in a group setting, you may want to divide your group into two smaller subgroups. One subgroup should prepare arguments for continuing with the counseling. The other subgroup should prepare arguments for not continuing. After your preparation, have your debate. What might be your personal conclusion?

7. Assume that you decide to continue with the counseling. What would be your counseling goals? What counseling approaches would you take?

8. Mr. D has heard voices on at least two occasions. He attends a church where it is an accepted part of their religious tradition to listen for the voice of God and to affirm those who hear God speaking audibly. What is the evidence that the voices that Mr. D hears are from God? What would suggest that the voices are a part of his mental disorder? What might suggest that the voices are satanic?

9. In preparing this case report, Mr. D's counselor mentioned that "this man had no attention as a child. Now as an adult he creates crises to get noticed." Give reasons why you would agree with the counselor or disagree. How would either of these (to agree or disagree) impact your counseling with this man?

10. Do you think it is safe to meet one on one with Mr. D? Give reasons for your answer. If you do not think it is safe, what would you do to protect yourself?

11. With all of the above in mind, what approach will you take when Mr. D arrives for his next appointment?

## General Questions

1. How would you respond to a church leader who would dismiss the case of Mr. D as evidence of sin in his life, and who would argue that the best treatment approach would be prayer, Bible reading, and encouraging Mr. D to be more obedient to God?

2. Discuss your thoughts about the role of demons in mental illness. What is the role of biological and neurological malfunctioning?

3. What are some ethical or moral implications of counseling with Mr. D? For example, do you have a responsibility to warn anybody about his occasional tendency to think violent thoughts? Could his church be encouraging the tendency to hear voices? If so, should you do anything about this? Do you have any responsibility to get medical attention for Mr. D?

4. What is the role of your church in meeting the needs of people with emotional disorders? What is your responsibility for helping your church to be more sensitive to mental disorders?

## Personal Reflection Questions

1. In the future would you like to counsel with people like Mr. D, or would you prefer some other kind of counselee? Give reasons for your answer.

2. At times probably all counselors see themselves in their clients. What is there about Mr. D that reminds you of behavior and attitudes in yourself? Have you ever heard voices, for example? Have you made impulsive decisions, had difficulty controlling your anger, misinterpreted innocent comments from others, or thought of harming another person or yourself? Does this raise discomforts in you or make you question your own stability? Reflect on this privately or in a journal. Then discuss it with one other person you trust, or talk about it with a counselor.

3. As you read the chapter on mental disorders in *Christian Counseling* did you wonder about your own stability or that of somebody you know well? Who would be a good person with whom to discuss these thoughts? When will you do this?

For a follow-up to the story of Mr. D, please go to the Epilogue at the end of the book.

# Alcohol-Related Problems

Helping people with substance-abuse problems can be a very rewarding experience. At times it can also be disheartening and frustrating. In describing the case that follows, the counselor wrote, "My experience in working with this population has taught me two truths. Things are not always as they appear on the surface, and you never want to remove something unless you can replace it with something better. Marjorie [whose story follows] helped me learn this lesson." As you read the counselor's description of this lady, see how these truths play out. Consider what you think would be an effective approach in counseling with her.

"Marjorie is a thirty-one-year-old, single, unemployed woman from Eastern Europe. She was referred by her probation officer for intensive outpatient group counseling after an arrest for drinking and driving. Marjorie allegedly passed out at the wheel and crossed the median into the path of an oncoming truck. Somehow the truck driver was able to swerve, but Marjorie hit a tree and woke up the next day in a hospital but with only minor injuries. Her blood alcohol content had been very high, almost three times the legal limit. In addition to DUI,* she also had been charged with possession of crack cocaine, which she had been using at the time of the accident. Previ-

---

* DUI is "driving under the influence" of alcohol or some other substance.

ously she had been picked up several times by police for seeking to buy drugs and for engaging in prostitution in order to support her habit. The judge gave her the option of either serving time in jail or going into treatment. She did not want to go to jail, so she chose the treatment.

"In the initial group session, Marjorie introduced herself and discussed her reasons for treatment. As she talked, there was something disturbing about the way she described herself as a "crack-head" and made statements more than once about how much she hated herself and felt like a bad person. As an aspiring counselor, I wanted to establish an early rapport, develop a platform of trust, and exercise a liberal amount of empathy and positive regard. I was determined to help this woman accept herself and break free from the bonds of her addiction. Although these intentions were good, I quickly realized that none of my formal school training had prepared me for what I was about to hear as Marjorie began to tell her story.

"There were reasons why she didn't like herself. She said that between ages eight and thirteen she had been sexually abused repeatedly by the various men her mother brought home. The mother was alcoholic and engaged in prostitution. Marjorie stated that she too was a mother. She had a ten-year-old daughter who had been adopted by Marjorie's sister because of the addiction. Even though she had not seen the child for nine years, Marjorie often thought about her and wanted to have a relationship with her, but she was ashamed and knew that the daughter would not have anything to do with an alcoholic mother. She knew, as well, that she was an unfit mother and felt terrible about it.

"When I asked Marjorie how she was able to cope with so much pain, she began to cry. She apologized and tried to hide the tears, but the group moved in to provide support and comfort. They reassured her that it was all right to cry and to show emotion, because it was probably long overdue. The group's response had a favorable effect and encouraged her to talk more. She said that this actually was the first time she had talked about this and that she felt safe. Marjorie confirmed my suspicion that her chemical use started around the same time as her abuse. She also spoke of what really happened the night of her accident and arrest. She said that she didn't pass out behind the wheel, but actually was trying to drive her car into the truck to end her life. She said she knows it was a miracle that she was still alive and believed that God kept her alive for a purpose. She needed to find relief from her guilt and past failure, establish new hope, and develop coping skills apart from alcohol and drugs so she could deal effectively with her life situations."

## Discussion Questions

1. Based on what you know about the causes of substance abuse, list the main influences in Marjorie's life that led to her addictions.
2. Is Marjorie's chemical use a cause or a result of her problems? Could it be both? Give reasons for your answer. How might your answer have an influence on the ways in which you would counsel Marjorie?
3. Would you urge Marjorie to stay in the group, to get individual counseling, or to get both types of treatment? What would be the advantages and disadvantages of each of these alternatives?
4. In the *Christian Counseling* book, Table 34–1 lists empirically demonstrated treatments that are effective in helping people who abuse alcohol. Which of these would you use with Marjorie?
5. If you were counseling Marjorie, what would be the first issue you would address? What might be next? Would there be issues you might have to postpone to a later time?
6. What would be your approach for helping Marjorie to stop abusing alcohol and using drugs? What would be your reasons for getting medical or other specialized help with this aspect of treatment? Are there reasons why you might not make a referral?
7. What is the evidence that Marjorie will stay with counseling and attempt to change? What is the evidence that she will not stay with treatment? How can you increase the likelihood that she will stay?
8. What suggestions would you make to give Marjorie more effective coping skills than alcohol and drugs?
9. How would you help Marjorie deal with her desire to see her daughter?

10. What biblical references and biblical principles might apply to Marjorie's case? In what ways can you apply biblical principles to Marjorie in order to facilitate her healing and recovery? Be specific.

## General Questions

1. What elements in the group helped facilitate Marjorie's acceptance of herself and ability to talk about her feelings? Why would it be important not to judge her but instead be willing to listen and give support as she explores her own issues?
2. What are likely to be the greatest challenges that you will face in helping Marjorie recover? How will you deal with each of these?
3. In what specific ways could a local church help Marjorie in her recovery?
4. Would you recommend that Marjorie join Alcoholics Anonymous? Why or why not?
5. At the beginning of this chapter, Marjorie's counselor wrote that there are two truths to remember in counseling substance abusers: things are not always as they appear on the surface, and you never want to remove something unless you can replace it with something better. Apply these two truths to Marjorie's life and treatment.

## Personal Reflection Questions

1. What is your personal experience in using alcohol and other chemical substances? Who do you know or who have you known who has had a problem with substance abuse? How has this influenced you? How might it influence your counseling with somebody like Marjorie? Discuss your answers with some other person that you trust.
2. What is the evidence, if any, that you could become an abuser at some time in the future? Does this question make you feel uncomfortable? If so, what are the reasons for this discomfort? What is the relevance here of 1 Corinthians 10:12–13?
3. What are your attitudes toward people who abuse alcohol? Do

these people threaten you, scare you, repulse you, arouse compassion in you, or stimulate other emotions? What are the reasons for these reactions? What is the evidence that they are biases? How will these attitudes influence your work in counseling with substance abusers? How could some of these attitudes be changed?

For a follow-up to the story of Marjorie, please go to the Epilogue at the end of the book.

# Addictions

The pages of this book include a remarkable collection of stories about people's lives and about healing through counseling. Most of these people have been introduced to us by their counselors, but a few have told their own stories. Perhaps no one has been more courageous and open than VT, age thirty, who talked about his life in a lengthy and poignant interview that is summarized in the following paragraphs.

"I have wasted a lot of years in my life. It started when I was only twelve. That was when I first experimented with marijuana. I stopped for a while but started again when I got into high school. That was also the time I started drinking on the weekends, most often with a friend who was a senior, planning to go to college. One weekend he was killed in a car accident. On the rebound I turned to a different crowd of friends, and the drinking increased. Even though I was against drugs, the kids at school knew me as the guy who could get marijuana. My dad was in ministry (he still is), but I did not want the life that my parents lived so I struggled a lot with who I was. I felt socially awkward and steeped in identity problems. I was most comfortable rebelling against school and my parents, but this involved more drinking and marijuana use. As I approached the end of high school, I started skipping classes, sitting around all day drinking and smoking marijuana. At about this time I also got into hallucinogens like LSD. I tried mescaline, and this really messed me up and had psychological effects that were far beyond my years of marijuana use. Eventually I was kicked out of school without graduating. My parents had no idea how to control me. I was very manipulative, and often would play the victim role that said 'You don't understand me. Leave me alone.' I acted like I didn't care, but I really did care. Inside I felt like a failure. I had let my parents down. They didn't know what to do. I had no accountability and no idea how to change.

"When it became clear that I would never get a decent job without a high school diploma, I got one by studying for a GED.* I had several jobs after that and always did OK, but by the time I reached twenty, my mind had been altered and I was an emotional basket case. I could be very funny, but inside I was wounded and in a lot of pain. I went to a counselor, where I would be broken up emotionally, but I refused to go when he wanted to send me to a long-term residential treatment setting. So I kept beating myself up emotionally, condemning myself because my parents were paying for treatment and I was not changing. During the days, I was a hard worker who had good opportunities for promotion, but more than once I quit when these opportunities arose. I was scared of any responsibilities, and sometimes I would drink myself out of any chance for advancement. After work my friends and I would sit around my apartment, do drugs, and drink. Eventually I began dealing drugs that I could get from a girl who stole them from the pharmacy where she worked. In my early twenties I had a girlfriend who one day said, 'If you want alcohol over me, I'm gone.' I let her go.

"While all of this was going on, I was getting more and more into pornography. It began when some neighbor kids introduced me to magazines and porn on television. For me this was an escape, and I told myself it was OK because my grandfather had *Playboy* and other magazines in the house. I was ashamed of my addiction and secretive about my solitary sexual activities, but I didn't stop.

"At this time in my life I wanted everything—sex, alcohol, drugs. I had always said that I would never use cocaine, but after my girl-

---

* GED (General Education Diploma) is a high school diploma that can be earned by adults who are past high school age.

friend left, I started hanging around bars and found that cocaine was big. I was only about twenty-two, doing cocaine, the one thing I said I would never do. I was hanging out with dangerous, gun-carrying drug dealers. My motives were dark, and I was trying to meet girls for the wrong reasons. At about age twenty-four I started hanging out with a guy who was into Satanism. He introduced me to methamphetamines, first through crystals that I put in coffee before I drank it. The dependency and side effects on my mind and body were horrible, ten times worse than cocaine. The second time I used crystal meth I got it from an old friend. As soon as I took it he shouted, 'Wow, now I have another customer.' This was highly addictive and dangerous, but I did meth seven or eight times.

"At this time in my life I was twenty-five years old and going down hill a hundred miles an hour. I was completely hooked on drugs. I was almost six feet tall but weighed only 130 pounds. I had used Ecstasy, cocaine, methamphetamine, and alcohol. One night I remember standing in my driveway. I stood there for about three hours, hallucinating, in a different world, 'wierded out,' a target for anybody who wanted to do anything. I had already been arrested once for driving under the influence (DUI) and twice for possession of marijuana. I had spent two weeks in jail where everybody was hooked on meth. Every conversation there was about crystal meth. I knew that I was on my way to death or prison. I had a brother who was successful in his career, but I had another brother who was addicted because of my influence. I felt guilty because I had corrupted his life. I still feel guilty. But at that point I decided not to do drugs anymore, so we called my probation officer to ask if I could have one last chance. My mother had done research on drug rehabilitation programs, so I was court ordered into a program that my mother had found. My parents took me for an interview, but as I sat there I had only one thought in mind: How I could get away for a Budweiser?"

## Discussion Questions

1. Assume that you are the first counselor to meet with VT and his parents. You greet them in your office and sit down to talk. Where will you start?

2. As you interview this family, what do you think might have been some of the causes of VT's drug addiction?

3. What might be some of the best ways to give treatment?

4. How do you think VT might be prevented from leaving the program and going for his Budweiser?

5. What does the Bible say about VT's addiction—its causes and cures?

6. In addition to a counselor, what other people might need to be involved in VT's rehabilitation?

7. In what ways should the parents and/or the family be involved with the treatment? Do the parents need treatment too? Give reasons for your answer.

## General Questions

1. As he got progressively involved with drugs, VT reported that his pornographic addiction lessened. For purposes of discussion, assume that the addiction to pornography was still significant. What might be the cause for this addiction? Assuming that VT was progressing in the treatment of his drug addiction, how would you go about counseling him for his addictions to pornography and sex?

2. Assume that you are trying to find a competent substance-abuse rehabilitation program for VT or his brother. Where would you find such a program? How would you make contact?

3. VT did not go to church even though his father was in ministry. In what ways could a local church help this family?

4. In what practical ways could counselors prevent addictions such as those that trapped VT?

## Personal Reflection Questions

1. What is there in your life that might make you vulnerable to becoming addicted to drugs, pornography, masturbation, Internet games, adrenaline, work, sports, or religion? What actions can you take to prevent this or other addiction? Discuss this with a friend or counselor that you trust.

2. Re-read the first sentence in the previous question. If your answer is "nothing," give reasons why you can be so sure that you will never become addicted. What is the relevance of 1 Corinthians 10:12–13?

For a follow-up to the story of VT, please go to the Epilogue at the end of the book.

# Financial Counseling

Christian counselors do not always feel comfortable helping counselees handle financial issues. This appears to be out of our areas of expertise—something for financial planners to handle. Despite this discomfort, concerns about money creep into the life stories of people who struggle with depression, anxiety, career choices, marriage problems, interpersonal conflicts, family issues, spirituality, and numerous other issues that people bring into the counseling room. For this chapter we turn to an experienced financial counselor who describes the case of a young married couple whose problems largely center on money.

Brad and Sue are a recently married couple with a three-month-old child. For the first time in their adult lives they have begun attending church because they want to lay a foundation for their new child. It is there that they signed up for a class in managing money along with the opportunity to meet with a financial counselor.

Brad is a salesman making over $50,000 per year, on average, and Sue is a stay-at-home mom. As a salesman, Brad's income has a high percentage of variable compensation that changes depending on how well he performs in his territory. So while he averages about $50,000 per year, month to month and year to year there can be significant swings in the amount of money that he earns.

Prior to his marriage, Brad developed a lifestyle that was based upon maintaining the perception that he was a successful businessman. In those times of financial plenty he lived richly. He bought a BMW sports sedan purchased with no money down on which he now owes more than the vehicle is worth. Together Brad and Sue also purchased a home that costs about 50 percent of his disposable income. In addition, credit card debt has been piling up, and Brad now owes more than $7,500 on his credit cards. Because of the current interest rates and finance charges, he is able to make only minimum payments each month. As a result, he holds over a large portion of the outstanding balances from month to month, paying the associated finance and fee charges, but doing little to reduce the balances that he owes.

This is Sue's second marriage. Her first husband had died in an accident about two years earlier, and she received an insurance settlement of over $500,000. Sue and Brad had met and married quickly, and had their child within a year of being married. To this point in their relationship they had not combined their assets or incomes. Sue and Brad had separate checking accounts, and managed all their finances independently.

Sue grew up in an affluent family and had been married to a man who was capable of meeting her accustomed lifestyle. She had been able to purchase nearly anything she wanted from the time she was very young. Through college her parents had provided her with a credit card and checking account and managed all these finances for her. She was very resentful of having to be in the counseling sessions. She felt that if Brad could just make more money and control his spending then they would not have to air their "dirty laundry" in front of a stranger.

Ultimately they came to financial counseling for very different reasons. Brad wanted to convince Sue that they should combine their assets and pay off the expanding consumer debt. It would save money for them as a couple, and relieve the stress they were having in their lives and increasingly in their marriage. Sue came to counseling to convince Brad that he needed to get his financial life in order. She wanted him to learn how to control his spending so that they did not spend through the insurance money and end up in the same situation in a few years. Ultimately Sue wanted to insure that she could stay home with their child and not have to worry about saving for college.

As their counselor you are put in the middle of a difficult situation. Both individuals have very good points to make. Financially Brad is correct that they would be better off as a couple in not having to pay the high interest rates of consumer credit. Sue is also correct that if they do not get their financial life in order they will be in the same situation in a few years after they spend the money from her insurance settlement. As the discussion continues, you discover that neither Brad nor Sue has any significant background in basic principles of money management or financial discipline. As people who are new to the church, they also lack any knowledge of biblical money management principles.

In the meantime the stresses are building within the marriage. Brad is feeling so much pressure that he has started to miss work because he is not feeling well. This absenteeism obviously is a significant problem for someone who works on commission. For Sue the pressure is creating distance from her husband. She is resentful and feels that he is not trying hard enough to correct the situation. They are looking to you for help.

## Discussion Questions

1. How do you start to counsel this couple without offending one or the other and causing one or both of them to back out of the counseling sessions?
2. Assuming that you are not a trained financial planner, would you refer Brad and Sue to a financial planner? Give reasons both for making a referral and for not referring.
3. What issues, financial and non-financial, are creating problems for Brad and Sue?
4. What would be your plan of action for helping this couple deal with their financial troubles? In giving your answer, draw on some of the suggestions in the section titled "Counseling and Financial Problems" in the *Christian Counseling* book.
5. Given your experience and level of training, would you try to help Brad and Sue establish and stick with a budget? Give reasons to support your answer.
6. Would you urge Brad and Sue to consolidate their finances and pay off the loans? Give reasons for your answer. Is there a different alternative? If so, what might it be and why is it better than the consolidation of resources?

## General Questions

1.  What would the Bible say about the causes of the financial problems that Brad and Sue are having? What are some key indicators that Brad and Sue are not following biblical instruction on finances?

2.  What would the Bible say about the solution to this couple's problems?

3.  This is a couple that has not attended church during their adult lives, and they are not familiar with any of the financial teachings of the Bible. For both Brad and Sue, giving is about putting any loose change from their pockets into the offering basket as it passes each Sunday. Give reasons why you, as a Christian counselor, will seek to impart biblical principles of financial management to a couple that has no awareness of this and perhaps little interest. How will you present these issues?

4.  List five key biblical verses that you could use to help Brad and Sue understand how the Bible is relevant to them and to their financial struggles.

5.  At what point should a financial counselor solicit help from a traditional counselor, and the traditional counselor solicit help from a financial counselor? Do you think one counselor can or should do both marriage and financial counseling, assuming that the counselor has the training?

6.  In addition to the financial counseling, do Brad and Sue need more traditional marriage counseling? Why or why not?

7.  How would you combine marriage counseling with counseling about their money management?

8.  Considering that these people are new Christians, how do you (a) urge them to tithe, (b) help them realize that God is loving and graceful even in the midst of financial struggles, and (c) give them reason for hope?

## Personal Reflection Questions

1.  Is it uncomfortable for you to be helping others with their financial problems? What makes you feel uncomfortable? How would this discomfort influence your counseling concerning financial issues?

2. As you have read this case and the chapter on finances in *Christian Counseling*, what issues have been raised about your own finances and money management? What needs to change?

3. In what ways are you following biblical principles in managing your own money? In what ways are you violating these principles? In what ways will you change? Who will hold you accountable as you make changes? When will the changes start? Be specific.

For a follow-up to the story of Brad and Sue, please go to the Epilogue at the end of the book.

# 37

# Vocational Counseling

Vocational problems can take a variety of forms. Sometimes the counselor helps a teenager select a college major or choose a vocational direction. At times, the focus will be on retired people looking for new directions after leaving their full-time careers. Other counseling will be with people who have been fired or released from their jobs because their companies have closed or merged and laid off their workers. The counseling principles are similar in most of these settings. The following paragraphs describe a successful company president who resigned from his job and then began a long struggle to find another position and maybe even another vocation.

When he was interviewed for this chapter, TL joked that his time with a business that we will call Local Software Company had been "a spectacular career-ending opportunity," but that isn't the way it all started. TL had graduated from college about twenty-five years ago, enrolled in a highly reputable business school, earned his MBA, and entered the business world. He brought all the qualities that would point to success: a good education, competence, the ability to speak well, good looks, sensitivity to other people, and appropriate social skills. He understood the world of business, learned from good mentors, and was devoted to his wife and his church. Opportunities for promotion came on a regular basis. TL enjoyed his work and put in long hours but never appeared to be driven or consumed by the workaholism that he saw in some of his colleagues.

The invitation to become the chief executive officer of Local Soft-ware Company came unexpectedly. It involved a significant promo-tion and salary increase, but it meant that TL and his family—which by this time included two preteen sons—would have to move across the country, away from family and church ties, and into a new com-munity. After prayer, reflection, and consulting with more experi-enced Christians and businessmen, TL and his wife agreed to make the move, and they started their new adventure with anticipation. When TL arrived at his new company, he was received enthusiasti-cally. Today he describes the first year in the new job as maybe the best of his career. He sensed the company's momentum, got involved with team building, saw initial growth under his leadership, and was thriving in his new employment.

Things started to unravel when two members of the executive team began to criticize TL's leadership. "I still can't figure out their reasons," TL said recently. "My guess is that they were jealous and probably did not like the changes that were being made. These two men were pretty traditional." Eventually, the critics began to talk to others, including board members, accusing TL of having motives or agendas that he did not have, systematically undermining his leader-ship, his credibility, and the trust that he had built within the com-pany. There was never any criticism of TL's character. There were no allegations of anything illegal, unethical, or immoral. Instead there were criticisms of his methods and his leadership style. To his credit, TL tried to deal with these rumors openly. He had meetings with the critics, gave reasons for his actions before the board, and later spoke at an employee meeting. When reports of unrest reached the media, TL cooperated with reporters and never dodged the issues or potentially embarrassing questions.

"But I could see that the ship was breaking up," TL stated. "I began to see why some people had told me that CEO really means 'career-ending opportunity.' I did not like the city where the Local Software Company was located, and my family was unhappy. Going to work was no longer fun or challenging. I felt tired and depressed. My wife and I began to have differences between us, probably brought on by the pres-sure. We went to a good counselor who helped, but the situation at work got worse." Long-time employees started to resign. Morale slid. There were factions that disagreed with each other, even on the company board. Some board members urged TL to stay the course and weather the storm. Others called publicly for his resignation.

Eventually, TL decided to leave, both for the good of his company and for the good of his family. Supported by a good severance package, TL and his family took a short vacation and then began the job search. The former CEO sent out resumes, hired a headhunter to locate new positions, searched the Internet for opportunities, and has had dozens of interviews. In every one of these the potential employer wants to know what happened at Local Software, and TL rehearses the details and also produces letters of recommendation from highly credible supporters. Every month that passes seems to make the search harder and raises more hesitation in the minds of potential employers who wonder "Why did this man leave such a good position, and why has he not been able to get another job?"

On the day of our interview for this book, TL was upbeat. "I am ready to jump back in the game," he said enthusiastically. "This has been tough. I was knocked down, but I can get back up. It has been good for all of us." But he admits that the experience has left him feeling defeated at times, depressed, insecure, angry, and struggling with identity issues. He wonders if he really is competent to be in business or if he should shift to a different career. He feels like he is having to start his career over again at age forty-seven. He still sees a counselor about once a month and takes anti-depressant medication on a regular basis. He and his family still attend church regularly, but they are adjusting to a new church. They felt the need to change churches after TL's resignation because some of the critics from his company were fellow worshipers who were spreading rumors about TL at the church where they all attended previously. At times, when he is alone or talking with his wife, TL reflects on what happened at his company, what he might have done differently, or where God has called him to serve at this point in his career. "I wonder at times who I am," he says. "I had twenty successful years in business before this. I'm not incompetent. But what happens now? Our whole family feels in limbo."

Assume that the counselor calls and asks if you could see TL for vocational counseling. The current counselor has helped TL with his marriage and has focused on the grief and emotional issues that have followed in the wake of the events at the Local Software Company.

According to the counselor, you do not need to focus on these more personal issues unless they arise, but you could help TL with his vocational choices and direction.

## Discussion Questions

1. When he enters your office, TL is cordial and gives no resistance to meeting with you. What will you do first in your meeting with him? Why?
2. List some goals for your counseling with TL.
3. What approach would you take in counseling with TL concerning vocational issues?
4. Review the section in the *Christian Counseling* book that deals with "Causes of Good and Poor Vocational Decisions." Which of these might you discuss with TL? Why would you focus on the issues that you have chosen?
5. Apply the Vocational Decision-making Process (see Figure 37–1 in *Christian Counseling*) to the case of TL.
6. What obstacles might be preventing TL from finding new employment? How would TL answer that question? What action could be taken to overcome these obstacles? Answer this question before reading further.
7. Review your answer to the above question. Did it occur to you that something or someone may be undermining TL's job search? For example, might there be a critical statement in one of TL's letters of recommendation that could be causing potential employers to back off? Might TL unconsciously be sabotaging his own job search? How could you help TL explore and deal with these possibilities?
8. TL is a committed Christian. Knowing this, in what ways will your counseling be different from the vocational counseling that might be done by a counselor who is not a believer?

## General Questions

1. Here is a quotation from Daniel H. Pink: "The Organization Man [who works all his life for the same big company] is history. Taking his place is America's new economic icon: the free

agent—the job-hopping, tech-savvy, fulfillment seeking, self-reliant, independent worker. These men and women are transforming America in ways both profound and exhilarating." What is the evidence that TL might function better working on his own, perhaps as a free agent, a self-employed business consultant? What are reasons for you to think that this kind of position would not be a good fit for TL?

2. What is the role of God's will in vocational counseling with Christian counselees? What is the place of God's will in vocational counseling with counselees who are not professed followers of Jesus Christ?

3. TL is discouraged. What would you do to give him hope?

4. How could you help TL avoid another crisis in his next position so that he does not repeat the experiences that led to his departure from the Local Software Company?

## Personal Reflection Questions

1. Please read this quotation from John Gardner: "What can be more satisfying than to be engaged in work in which every capacity or talent one may have is needed, every lesson one may have learned is used, every value one cares about is furthered?" For you, what kind of work would fit this description? Give reasons for your answer. Do you have this kind of work? If not, how could you move in this direction? Be specific in your answer. Will you move?

2. What are your strengths? How can these relate to your choice of a vocation? If you already are into your vocation, how can you utilize your strengths? What is the evidence that you are more fulfilled and effective vocationally and in other areas when you build on your strengths?

3. Apply the Vocational Decision-making Process (see Figure 37–1 in *Christian Counseling*) to yourself. Write out answers and discuss these with a trusted friend or counselor.

For a follow-up to the story of TL, please go to the Epilogue at the end of the book.

## PART EIGHT

# Concluding Issues

# 38

# Crises

Crises are a part of life. They disrupt our schedules, and they call for our attention. They reveal our character, and they shape who we are and who we become. Sometimes we see crises approaching; at other times they appear without warning. Some crises can be handled without assistance; others involve help from a counselor. The following story concerns a woman who worked in a counselor's office but who had symptoms of her own when a distraught counselee came for help.

Margaret is a forty-nine-year-old woman who works as the office manager and receptionist for a counseling center. She is consistently cheerful and able to relate to people, but one day an unpleasant incident with a client stimulated anxiety, flashbacks, and nightmares of a trauma that she had experienced twenty years earlier. Apparently the client had an anger-management problem and was not happy to learn that he would have to wait a few minutes because his counselor was behind schedule and running late for the session. The client started shouting at Margaret, who unexpectedly had a panic attack behind her desk at the clinic. Suddenly she had a flashback of her ex-husband stabbing her with a knife.

Margaret was surprised by this incident. She thought that her past crises had been resolved, but because of the incident in the waiting room, Margaret came to a counselor requesting an urgent appointment. She described how she had met her former husband at a Christian meeting when they both were students at a large East Coast university. He was studying medicine, while she was a literature major. After graduation, they got married at a big wedding, but the honeymoon did not last long. Margaret started noticing things about her husband, Mike, that she had not seen while they were dating. He was very controlling, and at times his anger escalated to the point where he would throw and break things around the house.

After the wedding, the couple moved to another part of the country where Mike began medical school. One year later, they had a baby, and Margaret stayed at home taking care of their little boy. In the meantime, the pressures of medical school seemed to increase and intensify Mike's angry outbursts, so Margaret decided to talk to her pastor. The pastor expressed his concerns, but he emphasized that it was important for a wife to submit to her husband. Shortly thereafter, Margaret and Mike had another child, and Mike decided to drop out of the medical school to work at a local company. For a while there was less tension at home, but then the outbursts returned with increasing frequency and intensity until Mike became physically abusive. Every time Margaret thought of leaving him, she was reminded by members of her church that God hates divorce and that wives should submit to their husbands.

Eventually, Margaret decided to see a counselor who focused on empowering her to become an independent and assertive woman. Margaret learned that she deserved to be safe along with her children, and she was encouraged to resist and refuse to tolerate any kind of abuse. A few months later, she decided to find a job and become financially independent so that Mike could no longer use money to control her life. One night, Margaret called the police because her husband was hitting her. Mike spent a day in jail and promised to change. He even started attending counseling sessions with his wife, but the abuse soon returned and Margaret finally filed for divorce. Many church members were not happy with her decision, but she determined to move forward. She also obtained a court order to protect her and her children since Mike threatened to kill her if she left him.

A month later, her husband broke into the new apartment, stabbed Margaret repeatedly, and left her in critical condition. Her children called the ambulance, and Margaret survived the attack, although she stayed in the hospital for several weeks recovering from her injuries. Mike was jailed for ten years, and Margaret moved to another part of the country to start a new life with her children. Soon after, she found a wonderful Christian man; they got married and continue to have a good relationship.

Although Margaret recovered from her physical wounds within a few months, the emotional wounds went deeper. For two years after that trauma, Margaret had nightmares and flashbacks of her husband stabbing her to death. She would wake up at night screaming for help. She also felt jumpy all the time. Her heart would start racing if someone knocked on her apartment door. She had a hard time focusing on her work, and sometimes her fellow employees and the people who came into the office complained that she was inattentive.

When she came for counseling after her panic attack in the office, Margaret said she was surprised at what happened because she thought that she had recovered from the trauma of the stabbing. Now, however, she is afraid that she might have to deal with these symptoms again. She is afraid that this trauma from many years ago will affect her life, work, and family.

## Discussion Questions

1. Assume that you are a counselor who works in the clinic where Margaret had her panic attack. You hear commotion in the waiting room and hurry to investigate. What would you do? How would you meet Margaret's immediate needs? Give reasons for your actions.
2. Suppose that the angry client in the waiting room is waiting for you. When you appear, he starts shouting at you like he shouted at Margaret. How will you deal with him even as you try to help Margaret?
3. Later that day, after she has calmed down, Margaret comes to see you in your office. How will you help her?
4. Long term, how can Margaret be helped to get past the current period of anxiety and to feel less worried about another panic attack in the future? Be specific in your answer.
5. Evaluate the guidance that Margaret got from the counselor before she filed for divorce. In what ways is this advice consis-

tent with biblical principles? In what ways, if any, is it inconsistent with what the Bible teaches?

6. Margaret is "afraid that this trauma from many years ago will affect her life, work, and family." How can you reassure Margaret realistically and help insure that her fears will not turn into reality?

7. Summarize the Christian principles that might be involved with this case. How do the Bible's statements about fear and anxiety apply (for example, see Philippians 4:11–13, 1 Peter 5:8, or 1 John 4:18)? Do you think Margaret needs to deal with emotions like anger or bitterness? What about the importance of forgiving the ex-husband who stabbed her?

8. Would you involve Margaret's current husband in your counseling? Why? Why not?

## General Questions

1. If Margaret is a fellow employee of the counseling center where you work, are there ethical issues that need to be considered before you counsel her? What are these issues? Should you refer Margaret to another counseling center? Give reasons why you should make a referral and why you would not refer. With this information in mind, what would you do about making a referral? Why?

2. Margaret thought she had recovered from the trauma of the stabbing. How do you explain the re-appearance of these feelings?

3. Why did the angry client arouse these feelings again?

4. Discuss the advice that Margaret got from her pastor and later from fellow church members. In what ways did this advice help Margaret and her situation? In what ways did it create harm? As a Christian, how would you use the biblical guidelines that the church members used? Would you simply overlook these guidelines? Why or why not?

5. Review the section in *Christian Counseling* on preventing crises. How can this apply to Margaret so that she does not panic the next time that angry client appears for his weekly appointment?

6. Margaret's children were present when their father tried to kill their mother. In what ways do you think this may have influenced the children? How could a counselor help these children who are now adults with families of their own?

## Personal Reflection Questions

1. What traumatic events have occurred in your life? How were you influenced by these events? What is the evidence that these events still have control over you (like memories of the stabbing still controlled Margaret)? How can you weaken this control by events from your past? Should you see a counselor about this? Why or why not? If so, who will you see and when?
2. What emotions came to you when you thought about a counselor rushing to the waiting room to calm Margaret and also to calm the angry client? What does this say about your potential to work as a crisis counselor?
3. What can you do now that will enable you to handle future crises with greater calm and competency? Be specific.
4. Some people seem more resilient than others. What about you? How will your degree of resilience impact your work as a counselor?
5. Think of those people who work with ongoing crises in prison camps or refugee facilities. How can you help these workers?
6. John Fawcett is a counselor who wrote these words:

> Aid workers, basically, have a pretty shrewd idea what they are getting into when they enter this career, and dirty clothes, gun shots at night and lack of electricity do not surprise them. Inter- and intra-agency politics, inconsistent management styles, lack of team work and unclear or conflicting organizational objectives, however, combine to create a background of chronic stress and pressure that over time wears people down and can lead to burnout or even physical collapse. Our findings suggest that strong relationships afford the best protection in traumatic and stressful environments.

What is the evidence for and against you becoming an aid worker who counsels?

For a follow-up to the story of Margaret, please go to the Epilogue at the end of the book.

# 39

# Trauma, Terror, and Terrorism

Terror (the state of intense fear) and trauma (the experience of intense stress) can have a highly disruptive influence on a person's stability, relationships, and daily functioning. Terrorists strive to create fear and trauma to advance their own political and religious agendas. Most often, however, terror and trauma occur because of events in life that are so distressing that they can trouble and immobilize people for years. What follows is a classic example.

Andre sat in the pastor's office with his face buried in his hands while his wife, Lourdes, sat distantly in a corner chair with her knees to her chest and a gaze fixed on the trash can by the door. Andre began by explaining his confusion and utter inability to support his wife after her behavior had changed about six months earlier. During a routine trip to the playground with their daughter, Hannah, Lourdes was talking to other mothers and temporarily lost track of the little girl. Quickly Lourdes became frantic and hysterical as she scanned the playground for her daughter. She grabbed other children from the playground and demanded that they tell her where her daughter was. The police were called, and, after an hour, they were able to locate Hannah down the street from the park playing on the swing set of a neighbor.

Despite a wave of relief that came over Lourdes at the discovery of her daughter, she continued to feel like she was in a constant state of panic. She began to stay home more often and frequently reported to

Andre that she did not feel safe. She avoided going to the park altogether with her daughter. Her sleep suffered because she constantly felt agitated, and when she was able to fall asleep, she would quickly awake to distressing nightmares. Andre noticed an abrupt change in her frequency of cleaning the house. He would come home from work and find her vigorously scrubbing and cleaning items in the house at the expense of playing with her daughter. In an attempt to console his wife, Andre reached out to her but was met with suspicion and emotional distancing. This was especially true when Andre attempted to initiate any form of sexual intimacy. Lourdes would frequently accuse him of using her as a sexual object to fulfill his sexual desires.

Lourdes grew up as an only child in a poor urban area of New York. Her mother was nineteen when Lourdes was born and had no extended family or friends to give support. To pay the rent, Lourdes' mother initially ran drugs but eventually moved to prostitution. By the time her daughter was nine, Lourdes' mother had become a serious heroin addict, and all the money she made as a prostitute was used to feed her addiction. The mother's drug supplier began to apply added pressure for her to meet her financial obligations and pay for the drugs that he was supplying, but she constantly was coming up short. After several aggressive beatings and threats by the supplier, Lourdes' mother succumbed to the only option he gave her: allow Lourdes to work as a child prostitute. An arrangement was made whereby Lourdes and her mother would go to the local park until paged by the supplier. Once paged, Lourdes and her mother would meet customers for sex in abandoned apartments.

Lourdes was able to break free of this lifestyle when police brought down the supplier in a raid. She was placed in a foster home until her mother received substance abuse treatment and got her life back in order. The foster family showed consistent love and displayed a lifestyle that was committed to following Jesus Christ. It was through this family that Lourdes gave her life to Jesus and began to rebuild the relationship with her mother.

Shortly before the incident at the park with her daughter, Lourdes had confided to her small group that she had been struggling with intrusive sexual thoughts. Specifically, she found herself daydreaming about engaging in anonymous sex with other men. Not coincidentally, these fantasies emerged whenever she was at the park with her daughter. It wasn't unusual for Lourdes to snap out of these thoughts and quickly whisk her daughter home. Lourdes never shared these thoughts with her husband, mostly out of fear that he would think she was crazy, but also because she wanted her history to stay in the past. However, as Lourdes sat in her pastor's office, slowly rocking in her chair, she knew that the past was invading the present.

## Discussion Questions

1. Assume that the pastor refers Lourdes and Andre to you for more in-depth counseling. What would you do when they arrived for the first visit? Give the reasons for starting in this way.
2. What are the causes of Lourdes' behavior, both when she was on the playground frantically searching for Hannah and currently? How will your answer impact the ways in which you counsel Lourdes and Andre?
3. What will be your counseling goals? Why?
4. Summarize the methods that you will use with this case. Explain your reasons.
5. Will you see Lourdes and Andre together? Will you see them separately? Will you use some combination of individual and couples counseling? Give reasons for your decision.
6. Lourdes and Andre are Christians. What difference will that make in your counseling?

## General Questions

1. What, if anything, does the Bible or Christian doctrine have to say about Lourdes' problems?
2. Explain how Lourdes' childhood experiences have influenced her and shaped her current behavior psychologically?
3. Explain how Lourdes' childhood experiences have influenced her and shaped her current behavior neurobiologically?

4. In what ways does this case illustrate post-traumatic stress disorder?

5. Give reasons why Lourdes could be helped by talk therapy and spiritual counseling alone. Give your reasons why Lourdes also might benefit from right-brain interventions such as art therapy or psychodrama? What methods, if any, would you use in addition to talking with Lourdes? Why?

6. How would you help Andre understand what is going on with his wife? Would you try to help Hannah cope with her mother's behavior? Give reasons for your answers.

7. What other people would you enlist to help you treat Lourdes? For example, how might you involve the pastor in the treatment? What about Andre? Hannah? Lourdes' small group? The other playground mothers? A physician who could prescribe medication? Give reasons why you would enlist the help of some people like these and not others.

## Personal Reflection Questions

1. After reading Lourdes' story and imagining yourself as the counselor, what are your initial reactions and feelings about working with this person?

2. Notice that Lourdes did not share any of her traumatic background with Andre because she was afraid he would think she was crazy, "but also because she wanted her history to stay in the past." Privately answer this question, perhaps with a pen and paper to write down your thoughts: *Are there any events in your past that are impacting you now but that nobody else knows about except God?* How has this event or events impacted you? What would be the advantages and disadvantages of talking about this part of your past with a counselor or trusted friend? If you share this part of your life, with whom would you talk? When?

3. What traumatic events in your past could influence your competence as a counselor at present and in the future? Record your answers on paper, but keep these notes in a secure place. What would be the benefits of sharing your conclusions with some other trusted person?

4. In times of widespread worry or concern over terrorism, in what practical way can you extend your knowledge about trauma and stress management to prevent terror, anxiety, or other problems among people in your church or community? Try to be specific.

For a follow-up to the story of Lourdes and Andre, please go to the Epilogue at the end of the book.

# 40

# Other Issues

Without any prior intention of doing so, counselors sometimes develop areas of specialization in which they become experts. The following story comes from a Christian counselor who works mostly—although not exclusively—with people who have eating disorders. As the story unfolds, however, we will see how most cases involve several issues other than the ones that brought the person to the counselor's office. When she came for counseling, Mary Ellen denied that she had a problem, but once she acknowledged her anorexia, other issues began to surface.

The Lee family is well respected in their upscale suburban community. Both parents are veterinarians, owners of an animal clinic that has served the community for over twenty years. The youngest of their two children, Shawn, twenty-two, calls himself the black sheep of the family because of his rebellious nature and minor run-ins with the local police. His twenty-eight-year-old sister, Mary Ellen, got married about three years ago and works part time as a medical technician. She came for counseling at her husband's strong urging, although she denied that she had a problem.

It did not take long for the counselor to conclude that Mary Ellen had "full-blown anorexia." She was obsessively concerned with exercising for hours every day, eating properly, and watching her calorie intake religiously. Mary Ellen had lost a lot of weight, but she took pride in her slim figure and would get angry and defensive whenever the counselor suggested that there might be an eating disorder. She refused to admit that she might have anorexia and vigorously resisted the counselor's recommendation that she get a complete physical examination at a center for eating disorders. When her husband and parents both agreed with the counselor, Mary Ellen reluctantly checked in to the eating disorder program, got the medical attention that was of critical importance, and continued to work with her counselor.

The counselee spoke in very positive terms about her parents and her husband. They are all Christians who have no inclination to be critical; the parents are encouragers who have always been cheerleaders for their kids. The parents were (and are) very supportive and never raised any questions whenever Mary Ellen would try new diets or appeared to be following unhealthy exercise programs. "I wanted them to say something," Mary Ellen told her counselor. "I wanted them to set some boundaries, to give me some guidelines—if only to show that they cared," but this never happened. She was torn between always pleasing them because they were so nice and doing something, anything, to get some structure. When she was a teenager, Mary Ellen dated some non-Christian men of questionable character, but the parents never raised any questions about these relationships. Today Mary Ellen thinks that her dating episodes and the acting out by her brother were both unconscious efforts to get the security that would have resulted if the parents had set limits. She was always the perfect child who kept her feelings and insecurities hidden. In contrast, Shawn externalized his problems, pushing the limits and being manipulative.

When she got married, Mary Ellen had a big wedding, but the honeymoon was a "horrible experience." Even though she had been physically active and had "fooled around" during her dating experiences, Mary Ellen had never had intercourse until her wedding night, and she found it to be painful and unpleasant. Even then, she concluded that there was something wrong with her body, and because of the discomfort the couple rarely has sex. She feels guilty about this and wonders if God is punishing her because of her premarital sexual experimentation.

Having been through the eating disorder program, Mary Ellen slowly came to accept the fact that she had a problem. She had always been a perfectionist, compulsive and consistently scrupulous about her body, her faith, her work, and her marriage. She recognized that her husband had been unusually patient and supportive, but the eating disorder had become her real source of security. She had learned to keep her feelings and her inner thoughts to herself, hidden behind an "everything is fine" façade. Her husband, her parents, and even God were not let into her life. Once she let down her guard and told the people in her small group about the eating disorder. Immediately she felt a sense of shame, and whenever she walked into church, she would think that others were looking at her and that "everybody knew" about her problem. Before long, the couple moved to another church, but they are minimally involved. Mary Ellen doesn't mention her faith much. She has told the counselor that she struggles with her prayer life and has difficulty finding the time to read the Bible.

## Discussion Questions

1. Mary Ellen has a very capable counselor who makes it a practice to meet on occasion with a supervisor who can give an outsider's input into how the counseling is developing. Assume that you are that supervisor. The counselor tells you the above story and then asks "How am I doing?" What would be your answer?
2. Look at Table 40–1 in the *Christian Counseling* book. What is the evidence that Mary Ellen has an eating disorder?
3. What are the main causes of Mary Ellen's eating disorder?
4. In what specific ways have the parents, the husband, and Mary Ellen herself contributed to the onset and the continuation of the anorexia? What has each done to help solve the problem?
5. Mary Ellen has kept her feelings locked within herself. How could a counselor help her acknowledge and share her feelings in healthy ways? Be specific.
6. List some specific goals for working with Mary Ellen. Would you involve her husband in this process? Why and how?

## General Questions

1. The counselor appeared to be very determined about getting Mary Ellen to go for a physical examination by medical person-

nel who understand eating disorders. Why do you think this
was so important?

2. In describing her work with Mary Ellen, the counselor mentioned that the husband tends to be overweight and not at all
concerned about his high cholesterol, high blood pressure, and
snacking on unhealthy fast foods. In his job as an accountant,
however, he needs to be highly structured. What influence, if
any, might these facts about the husband have on Mary Ellen's
disorder and on the recovery?

3. What is the evidence, if any, that tensions could be brewing
between Mary Ellen and her overtly supportive husband? How
might these issues be raised in counseling?

### Personal Reflection Questions

1. Do you know anybody with an eating disorder, including obe-
sity, anorexia, or bulimia? If so, how does knowing this person
influence the ways in which you might counsel somebody like
Mary Ellen?

2. Think about your own eating habits? In what ways might you
have an eating problem or eating disorder? What can you do
about this? When will you take action and who will hold you
accountable?

3. Look over the topics in chapter 40 of the *Christian Counseling*
book. Where do you see yourself in this chapter? Where do
you need to make some personal changes? How and when will
you make these changes?

4. Are there any sections of chapter 40 that made you feel
uncomfortable, perhaps wanting to avoid the people in one of
the groups that you were reading about? Talk about these feelings with somebody that you know and trust. How might these
feelings impact your work as a counselor?

For a follow-up to the story of Mary Ellen, please go to the Epilogue
at the end of the book.

# 41

# Spiritual Issues

Of all the cases in this book, the hardest to find and the last to be written was the story of Bonnie that follows. Perhaps every issue that is brought to a Christian counselor is, in some way, a spiritual issue. In contrast, every explicitly spiritual problem that you might encounter is likely to have other issues involved as well. Certainly that is true of Bonnie, who had what her counselor called a combination of spiritual and psychosocial issues.

Bonnie is forty-eight, divorced, a single mom with three kids, all of whom have been diagnosed with attention deficit disorder. She grew up in a Christian family that regularly attended a fundamentalist church where Bible teaching was emphasized and the people were caring, but the expectations for church members and their children tended to be rigid. Bonnie wanted to be a ballerina, and the many years of training and practice shaped her into a good dancer. In some ways, however, the ballet training was similar to what she heard at church and at home. She had a teacher who used ridicule, demeaning public comments, and sarcasm in an effort to shape his young dancers. There was a constant demand for perfection. Bonnie and the other dancers were told again and again that they were not good enough, and they began to believe that they could never be good enough. Maybe the teacher thought that his students would be motivated by condemnation, but instead they were increasingly demoralized. Deeply ingrained in Bonnie was a belief in her own lack of worth.

As a young woman Bonnie married a non-Christian who was described as a "nice guy" but who nevertheless was immature and very much addicted to pornography. Almost from the beginning Bonnie felt guilty about her marriage to a nonbeliever, and the guilt and self-blame increased significantly when the couple divorced and her ex-husband moved to another part of the country, leaving Bonnie to raise the children. Periodically they go to visit their father for a week, and Bonnie plunges into her business with special intensity while the kids are gone. She is competent in her work and has been described as a great salesperson, but the children make a lot of demands on her time, so relaxation is not a regular part of her lifestyle.

A personal crisis arose when Bonnie decided to take time off for herself during a week when the children were gone. She dreamed about relaxing and getting refreshed, but quickly she discovered that there was nothing to do. She started thinking about her life overall, about her failures, her unwise decisions, her shattered marriage, her lack of self-confidence as a parent, the deadness of her spiritual life. Her mind began to dwell on her self-criticisms, doubts, and anger at what she had done with her life and failed to do. Away from her work and children, alone with herself, Bonnie was inundated by self-defeating thoughts that were pulling her down, overwhelming her with worries, and reinforcing her innate self-loathing. In the office of her counselor she said that she was worried about her faith. She described an increasing struggle to motivate herself to read the Bible, and she reported a significant slump in her prayer life. For the past several years she has attended a church that is less oppressive than the one where she grew up, but worship services have begun to bore her. "I can't seem to feel God's presence," she said. "I know I am not growing spiritually. I can't find words to say in prayer. It seems like God isn't there any more. What's wrong with me?"

### Discussion Questions

1. What *is* wrong with Bonnie? What is causing the negative thinking in her life? Be specific.
2. What is causing the spiritual struggles in her life?
3. In what ways have Bonnie's early experiences shaped her spirituality?

4. Based on your answers to the previous two questions, what would be your goals in helping Bonnie? What would you do first? Why?

5. Like her children, Bonnie has been diagnosed with attention deficit disorder. What might be the role of this disorder in understanding and helping Bonnie deal with her problems?

6. What psychological/counseling methods could be of help to Bonnie? What spiritual interventions would be helpful? Which would you use with Bonnie? Why?

## General Questions

1. In helping Bonnie, what, if any, might be the role of spiritual disciplines such as prayer, meditation, worship, fasting, service, or study? Which spiritual disciplines would be most helpful? Which ones, if any, might make the problem worse?

2. What is or should be the role of the church in helping Bonnie? As a counselor, what would you recommend?

3. Re-read the following quotation from the *Christian Counseling* book: "In the midst of this environment [where we live], a number of deeply committed believers sincerely want to serve God and to grow as Christians, but they struggle with discouragement and a lack of spiritual vitality. These people know that dynamic Christian living is possible, even in a culture that is only superficially religious. They long for a vital Christian spiritual life, even though many are unsure what that means and most have no idea how to get it." To what extent is that a description of Bonnie? How can Christian counselors help others overcome a lack of spiritual vitality and experience dynamic Christian living? Be specific in your answer.

## Personal Reflection Questions

1. Is there anything about Bonnie's story that describes you? To what extent are you like the people described above, "deeply committed . . . sincerely wanting to serve God and grow" as a Christian but struggling with a lack of spiritual vitality, longing for a vital Christian life but with no idea how to get it? Be hon-

est with yourself and before God as you answer. To the extent that you lack spiritual vitality, what can you do to change? Be specific? If you do not want spiritual vitality in your life, what might be the reasons for this? This is another one of those personal reflection questions that can make a big difference in your life and your future effectiveness as a Christian counselor.

2. Take time to write a self-evaluation of your own spirituality. Consider discussing this with a counselor, sensitive friend, or spiritual advisor. With whom would you discuss your own spiritual life? When? If you cannot think of a person, reflect on the reasons why.

3. In what ways will your spirituality influence the ways in which you do spiritual counseling?

4. Are you willing to pray with clients, meditate with them, read the Bible with them, worship with them, allow the Holy Spirit to guide your time with clients? Be honest about any hesitations that you might feel using spiritual interventions such as these. Talk with God about these insecurities. Would there be value in discussing them with a Christian friend? Why would you have that conversation, and with whom would you talk?

For a follow-up to the story of Bonnie, please go to the Epilogue at the end of the book.

# 42

# Counseling the Counselor

Most counselors are compassionate, caring people. They freely give to others and make themselves available to people in their times of need. In contrast, it can be extremely difficult for counselors to attend to their own needs for nurturance, rest, balance, and renewal. Why do so many burn out? Why is it so difficult for us to care for ourselves as we care for others? What follows is the honest confession of one of the counselors who provided some cases for the earlier chapters of this book.

"I grew up in a Christian home where I was taught the importance of serving others. My family modeled this, so it wasn't surprising that I went on to choose a helping profession. Besides, being a counselor fit who I was as a person. By nature, I tend to be pretty intuitive and sensitive, and I've always been the person that everyone talked to about their problems. I was still in high school when I decided to be a counselor. Even then I had been given a particular burden for children who have been abused and neglected.

"My first experience with such children was when I took an internship for my psychology major in college. I still remember the forty-five-minute drives back to campus after a long day on internship. I would cry the whole way. I couldn't separate myself from the pain of the children with whom I worked. By the time I got through the required years of college and graduate school to become a psychologist, I had learned better to cope with being exposed to such evil and such sorrow. I had begun to learn the art of emotional distance.

"The tougher challenge by far is the one with which I still struggle: learning the limits to my helping. It has been my nature to take on more than I can handle, to give more than I can afford. It's hard to slow down when your work carries such weight, when you're entrusted with the care of young souls. Certainly there's nothing wrong with caring deeply, but there's a fine line between opening yourself up to be used by God and feeling (albeit unconsciously) that God can't do it without you. I know. I've been on the wrong side of that line on more than one occasion. In fact, I'm there right now.

"Currently I work in a leadership role at a nonprofit agency. My occupation involves working with children who struggle with severe emotional and behavioral problems as a result of being abused and neglected. My job is 24/7, plus about eight more hours on top of that. The work is never done. It seems like the needs are never met. I rarely get a break, and when I do, I feel guilty. I know this isn't true, but I feel like things will fall apart without me. Lately, my health has begun to decline. I have been suffering from a variety of ailments and have been poked and prodded by more than one doctor. The final diagnosis is always the same: too much stress. I know it's true, but even as a trained counselor I don't know how to stop. Lately, I will cry at anything. I have begun to cry even at work. This has been most embarrassing. But I feel so raw all of the time, so moved by the needs.

"At church on Sundays, the pastor has been talking about the many roles that God plays. Last week, as he was talking about God as a loving father and best friend, I began to cry. I was overwhelmed by the thought that God could love me that way. I know intellectually that God loves me, but on a personal level this hasn't seemed to connect with where I am. Somehow, in my desire to share God's love with others, I had forgotten that he loves me as well. Somehow I have come to see myself as the person that God uses to reach out to others rather than a person that God reaches out toward."

## Discussion Questions

1.  If this counselor were your friend, telling this story to you over coffee, what would you do to be helpful?
2.  In what ways, if any, would you do anything different if the

person who told this story came to you for counseling?

3. What are the reasons for the stress that this counselor is experiencing? How would you help the person deal with these issues? Be specific.

4. Review the section on "The Counselor's Spirituality" in the *Christian Counseling* book. How can this be applied to this case?

5. The counselor made this statement: "even as a trained counselor I don't know how to stop." How would you help this counselor stop, slow down, and feel less pressured? How would you apply this advice to yourself? Be specific.

6. The counselor made no mention of family, friends, or others who can give support. In what specific ways can other people give support and help to this burned-out people helper?

## General Questions

1. Respond to this statement: *We increase the risk of burnout when we stop depending on God to guide our work and depend instead on our own strength.* What are some of the indicators when Christian counselors stop depending on God and are depending instead on their own efforts? What is the evidence that the counselor in this case has stopped depending on God? In what specific ways could you help this counselor to make changes?

2. Give your reaction to the following quotation from Richard Exley.

   We must live God-centered, God-directed lives, not need-centered lives. Compassion born only out of sympathy for suffering humanity risks both the extremes of fanaticism and burnout. . . . If our only motivation is need, we will be swallowed up, we will risk becoming part of the problem rather than part of the solution. Our only hope is to let God define our area of responsibility and then to live within our limits, both emotionally and physically.

3. How does this apply to counselors? In practical ways, how do you define your area of responsibility, before God, and then live within these limits?

## Personal Reflection Questions

1.  Unlike many of the other cases in this book, this one can apply to counselors and other readers personally. Read the case again and think how it might describe you. What does that mean for your counseling? What does it say about changes that need to be made in your life?

2.  Review the section on "The Counselor's Spirituality" in the *Christian Counseling* book. In practical ways, how can this be applied to you?

3.  What are you doing to keep relevant in your counseling work? Please be specific. What other things could or should you be doing?

4.  If your life ended within the next few days, what legacy would you have left? What can you do now to change the legacy that you will leave behind?

5.  Based on your understanding of the reasons for counselor stress, what specific changes do you need to make in your life and work? Write these down. Use Table 42–1 in *Christian Counseling* as a guide. With whom will you share what you have written? When will you start to make changes, and who will hold you accountable? If the list is long, where will you begin? (Remember that if you try to do too much all at once you are more likely to fail.) Please do not neglect this exercise. For you, this could be the most important response that you will make as a result of reading this book.

For a follow-up to the story of this counselor, please go to the Epilogue at the end of the book.

PART NINE

# Future Issues

## 43

# Counseling Waves of the Future

The final chapter in *Christian Counseling: A Comprehensive Guide* raises a number of issues that move beyond traditional counseling. To illustrate these, we are presenting the stories of two people who have come for counseling. The first describes a young man who attends an emergent church and whose background reflects postmodern and technology issues that may not be seen in counselees who are older, attending more traditional churches, or living in communities where the following influences may be less apparent. Kevin reflects some characteristics of his generation, but he is not typical of his generation. Nobody is. Every counselee is unique, and every problem issue is unique and able to teach us further about counseling.

## CASE STORY 1—Kevin

Kevin is twenty-three, an active participant in his emergent-style church and a young man who freely admits that there have been "tons of garbage" in his life. He grew up in a home where he had no sense of feeling anchored. His mother has had a variety of jobs and likes to spend time getting together with her friends. His dad works in a garage and has been detached from his family for as long as Kevin can remember. The parents have given no moral direction to their children, have let them do what they want, and have left Kevin and his siblings to find their own beliefs, even though the parents occasionally attend a local church.

As a teenager, Kevin got heavily involved using and selling drugs. He often attended raves* and quickly got into a promiscuous lifestyle. He has experimented with a number of different spiritualities and eventually had a radical conversion to become a follower of Jesus. "I need Jesus," Kevin told his pastor. "Jesus has rescued me. He is my healer and deliverer. Jesus sets me free." Kevin entered a drug rehabilitation program but quit because the people did not talk about Jesus and the program was not spiritual enough. He has been drug free for several months, but Kevin resisted the program leaders' demand for accountability and practical life changes. "I don't need medication, or programs, or practical things to do or going to a counselor." Kevin said. "I've got Jesus."

Kevin also has a lot of inconsistency in his life. He talks about serving Jesus and seems to be genuine in this desire, but he is involved in pornography, sex shops that sell sexually arousing products, sexually explicit conversations with strangers on the phone and Internet, and promiscuous sexual behavior. He can be actively enthusiastic in evangelism, but he also can yell and swear using foul language. He wants clear, concise, almost dogmatic answers to his theological questions, but he resists authority, legalism, and accountability. He makes promises and commitments but rarely follows through. He claims to have strong beliefs and says he wants strong leadership, but, according to the pastor, "nailing down what Kevin thinks and believes is like nailing Jell-O." He also tends to fight the normal realities of life. For example, he believes that settling into a job or building a career is "selling out and not following Jesus wholeheartedly." He has been to several counselors but rarely stays with one very long. These experiences have taught him a lot about counselor skills, and sometimes he feels that he is more knowledgeable about counseling than his counselors.

The pastor describes Kevin as being "completely digital, probably digitally addicted." From the time he wakes up until he goes to bed, Kevin is checking his email messages, connecting with other people, surfing the web, listening to music, and playing games. He appears to

---

* Raves were discussed in chapter 35 of *Christian Counseling*. These are all-night dance parties where participants take Ecstasy to produce feelings of well-being, high energy, stimulation, sensory distortions, and intoxicating experiences.

medicate himself with stimulation that he can control. As a young man who has had almost no controls on his life, Kevin often feels out of control, overwhelmed by life, and unable to manage himself. One thing he can manage and control is the input of stimulation. When he plays games or communicates with other people, he gets immediate feedback and is able to respond without waiting. He admits that he can't get enough of digital gaming. A church service is too long for him unless he can respond in some way or connect with others digitally even during the service.

Kevin assumed that when he became a Christian his life would be more under control, but this has not happened. He has trouble working with people, tolerating their personality differences, or allowing them to think in terms that are not black or white. He needs a spiritual community, but he goes from church to church, joining different groups, and then leaving them because he feels so ashamed of his life and so guilty because he has grieved the Holy Spirit.

## Discussion Questions

1. The pastor would like you to meet with Kevin and be his counselor. What would be reasons for agreeing with this request? What would be reasons for not becoming Kevin's counselor?

2. If you did become Kevin's counselor, what actions would you take to insure that you do not become the latest in Kevin's series of unsuccessful counselors?

3. Review Kevin's background. What obstacles will need to be overcome if the counseling is to be successful? How will you intervene to help Kevin overcome these obstacles?

4. As a Christian counselor, will you insist that Kevin stop his promiscuous behavior and/or his involvement with pornography? Give your reasons. If these behaviors are to be stopped, how will this happen? Be practical in giving your answer.

5. Kevin grew up in an age dominated by technology, especially digital technology. Since he likes to be digitally connected and in control, how might this hinder your counseling?

6. In what ways could you use Kevin's interest in technology to increase the likelihood of success in your counseling? How could you and Kevin use technology to help him get better

control of his out-of-control life? What are the advantages and disadvantages of using technology in these ways?

7. List reasons why you can have hope for Kevin.

## General Questions

1. Look at the final chapter of the *Christian Counseling* book. How many of the ten waves of the future do you see in Kevin's life? In what ways would this impact your counseling?

2. Summarize what you know about postmodernism. What evidence of this do you see in Kevin? How will this influence your counseling? In what ways is your counseling with Kevin likely to be nontraditional?

3. Kevin's pastor made the following statement: "If I have a model for ministry, it is community. The people in our church are all messed up, but we are in community. The people who have made it and grown spiritually and personally are those who have stayed in community. We have to have a community of nurture. We study the Bible and learn in community." What is the likelihood that Kevin will stay with this community? Give reasons for your answer. How could you use this community perspective to help in your counseling with Kevin?

4. What are some practical ways in which you as a counselor could help the pastor counsel with people like Kevin?

5. What are some expressive therapies that might work with Kevin? Which of these might you use and why?

6. Do you agree that Kevin needs to be involved in a church or other community? What would this community give him? How might community hinder him? Give your reasons.

7. What might be the best type of church for Kevin? Is the emergent church best? What about a pragmatic/seeker-sensitive, purpose-driven, or traditional church?

## Personal Reflection Questions

1. What might be the best type of church for you? Is the emergent church best? What about a pragmatic/seeker-sensitive, purpose-driven, or traditional church?

2. The pastor believes that Kevin and everybody else needs to be connected with a strong community if there is to be growth. Is this true of you? Give reasons for your answers.

3. Is there anything about Kevin that you admire? What might be reasons for this admiration? How might this influence your counseling? Be selective in choosing people with whom you might share your answers to these questions.

## CASE STORY 2—Nadette

This book has focused on the stories of people who most often live in stable communities and who voluntarily go to counselors for help with problems. In contrast, Nadette was born in a country that has been torn apart by civil strife and intense violence. She is not unique. Probably there are several million young people like her. They live lives of desperation and almost never get the help that Christian counselors can give. I hope that Nadette's story will expand your knowledge about counseling. Maybe it will even motivate some readers to take their counseling skills to worlds that few of us will ever know.

Nadette was eleven years old when the rebels raided the village where she and her family were living. The rebels were known for the atrocities they committed against civilians, including murder, rape, amputations, and abductions. Nadette and her family escaped to a nearby village, which the rebels soon attacked. The family escaped again to another village, but when the rebels attacked they killed both of her parents. Nadette was terrified of them, but she also was alone. Like so many other children who face similar circumstances, Nadette chose to join the rebels, in part for her own protection and survival.

For four years, Nadette lived with the rebels. She participated sometimes as a "camp follower" doing chores typically associated with being female. She also learned how to use a gun and participated in activities that the rebels were well known for—burning down villages, killing important people, stealing. She never admitted to anything specific, but Nadette was part of a group that forced young rebels to torture their own people. Those who refused knew the consequences: they likely would be severely beaten or even shot. She had seen this happen more than once.

Nadette had not been long in captivity when she was raped and became pregnant. The baby that she gave birth to in the bush died, and soon after that the rebel that impregnated her also died. Whereas before she at least had been safe with one man, now she was alone and unprotected. She managed to escape when the rebels attacked a large city and were driven out. Eventually she found refuge in a displaced person's camp, but life there was no better. The camp conditions were deplorable, but she had no place else to go.

At the camp, Nadette became involved with a man who impregnated her, but not long after she had the baby, he left her and the baby to fend for themselves. For a girl who grew up surrounded by family and kin, she was now in a setting without immediate or extended family. On top of that, she had a child to care for and had little hope of finding someone to take care of her. If she were at home in her village, she would have the support of her family and other relatives to help her care for the baby. Of course, that would have been under different circumstances.

Today, three years after her arrival in the camp setting, Nadette is still there. She believes that she would be welcome if she could get back to her village, but the counselor who talked with Nadette wonders. "She has too many cultural strikes against her," the counselor wrote. "She joined a group that was hated and feared. Initially raped, she is now tainted, and, in addition to that, she presently is caring for an illegitimate child, whom many would assume to be a 'bush baby.' At first she was a victim, but she also has been a perpetrator. She was a victim of the rebels, of abduction, of the rape. She has been a perpetrator of violations against her own people, and she has violated her own conscience as well. To complicate the issue, she has no education, no way to improve her lot, nothing to offer her family or kin or community if she were to return, and she is not even sure that there actually is a place to which she could return. If she does not find a hopeful solution to her practical problem of making a living and raising a child, she may feel forced into prostitution. At least this pays. However, if she thought she knew exile before, a life of prostitution certainly would seal her fate."

## Discussion Questions

1. Nadette's story is included in the chapter on future issues because twenty-first-century counseling could increasingly involve new methods and problem issues like those that Nadette faces. But this case also draws on themes from many of the previous chapters in this book including young adult-hood, grief, anxiety, sexuality, conflict, depression, loneliness, violence, abuse, family issues, trauma, and terrorism, to list a few. With all of this in mind, where would you start if you were a counselor in the refugee camp, seated in front of Nadette, and wanting to be of help?

2. What would be your counseling goals? Why would you choose these goals and not others?

3. What makes Nadette's case unique? How does this complicate your work?

4. How would you deal with each of the following questions that came from the writer of this case after she met with Nadette:

   - Since Nadette was abducted at such a young age, is she responsible for her actions? How will your answer impact your counseling?

   - In non-industrialized nations, childhood is viewed differently from the way it is viewed in more developed countries. Nadette comes from a culture where one is considered adult when one reaches child-bearing age. Does this make her more responsible or accountable for her actions? If so, what difference does that make?

   - Nadette committed acts that significantly violate her culture. Is she guilty? Does she need forgiveness? If so, how can you help her find forgiveness? What makes you think that she might hold herself responsible?

5. Nadette is not a Christian. How can you help her through Christian counseling?

6. Shift your attention to the relief workers, counselors, and people like them who work in the refugee camp and try to help people like Nadette. What are their struggles? What puts them under pressure?

7. How can you help these people? Be practical and specific.

## General Questions

1.  Talk therapy is not likely to be of much help to Nadette. What would help? Be specific.
2.  Would it help to read the Bible to Nadette? Give reasons for your answer.
3.  Nadette is from a group culture. How do you think that relates to counseling with Nadette or with other people in similar settings? Who from her group should be involved in helping her?
4   As a foreigner, how might you facilitate help for Nadette? How might the fact that you are a foreigner interfere with treatment?
5.  What further training or experience would you need to help Nadette or the overburdened relief workers who care for people in her camp?
6.  What would be the arguments for and against bringing Nadette to a developed country where she could live in better conditions and with greater security?

## Personal Reflection Questions

1.  How has the case of Nadette impacted you? Be specific.
2.  Do you have a tendency to read this case, feel overwhelmed, experience compassion for Nadette, and then pass on to cases that seem more relevant to your situation? How do you explain your reaction?
3.  Read and ponder Luke 10:30–37. Think about the priest, the Levite, and the modern Christian counselor.
4.  What, if any, might be your future role in helping people who are like Nadette or those who care for people in refugee camps and similar places? What about immigrants or other people who are struggling to adjust to living in your own community? If you have no sense that you should get involved personally with people like this (not everyone is called to this kind of work), how might you assist others who might feel called or want to get involved? Once again, please give specific answers.
5.  In what ways can the earlier chapters of the *Christian Counseling* book help with this case?

6. In what ways can the last chapter of the *Christian Counseling* book apply to both Nadette and Kevin?

For a follow-up to the stories of Kevin and Nadette, please go to the Epilogue at the end of the book.

# 44

# Conclusion

One of the most moving stories in the Bible concerns a young man named Joseph. Initially immature, insensitive, and seemingly self-centered, Joseph so alienated his eleven brothers that they sold him into slavery and faked his death. While they went on with their lives, Joseph was taken to Egypt, where he was sold to the captain of Pharaoh's guard, given unusual opportunities to lead, falsely accused of rape, thrown into prison, apparently forgotten, then rescued and miraculously appointed the number-two man in all of Egypt.

One day Joseph's brothers arrived at the palace asking to buy food in a time of devastating famine. The years had passed, appearances had changed, and they did not recognize Joseph, but he knew who they were and eventually revealed his identity to the astonished siblings. As the famine continued, all of Joseph's brothers and their families came to live in Egypt, along with their aging father Jacob. After their father died, the brothers feared that Joseph would get revenge for "all the evil they had done" when they sold their young brother into slavery many years before. Instead, Joseph told them not to be afraid. "As far as I am concerned," he said in a kind and reassuring voice, "God turned into good what you meant for evil. . . . No, don't be afraid. Indeed, I myself will take care of you and your families" (Genesis 50:19–21).

The preceding pages of this book describe the stories of more than sixty people whose lives have known pain, sorrow, confusion, and sometimes conflict. For some of these people, the pain continues and so does their counseling. For others, things have improved. Many of these people have seen God's hand at work in their lives, like Joseph saw God at work. What others may have meant for evil, God has turned into good. The lives of these people are stories of hope.

Princess Kasune Zulu is another story of hope. A newspaper reporter described her as "possibly the most inspiring and noble woman I have ever met.... You are infected by her warmth as she enthusiastically grabs your hand and smiles from the depths of her heart, while communicating her cause with her eyes before she has a chance to verbally." Princess is her Christian name and not a title, but she has a royal lineage and shows many of the attributes that we might expect to see in royalty: beauty, poise, social grace, and an awareness of the needs of her home-people.

My daughter introduced me to Princess Zulu one morning when they were sitting together in church. I learned that Princess was born in Central Zambia, into a family that has been torn apart by AIDS. Her parents died as a result of the disease, and so did her sister, a brother, and numerous friends and cousins. Left to survive with her three siblings after the parents had died, Princess was forced to drop out of school, and at age eighteen she married a man who was more than twice her age. Eventually Princess Zulu discovered that she and the man who is now her former husband were both HIV-positive. This news could have been a cause for despair. Instead, God turned it into good.

Shortly after hearing her diagnosis, Princess began speaking about the AIDS epidemic and the forty-two million people who live with the disease. In a world where secrecy about AIDS still abounds, Princess speaks boldly about her disease and her hope in Christ. She is passionate in describing how entire communities have been ravaged by the HIV epidemic and how millions of children are without parents, forced to work in order to survive, sometimes living on the streets where they have the potential to become hardened and open to involvement in criminal activities. These children feel neglected by society. They don't belong to anybody and are not sure where they fit. In her role as an international spokesperson and AIDS educator for World Vision's Hope Initiative, Princess Zulu has taken her message to huge arenas, to presidents and political leaders in the highest levels of government, to academic audiences, and to church leaders. But she shows the same passion and gracious spirit in talking with visitors to a church, with small groups of high school kids, or with individuals that she meets in her travels. "World Vision and the Hope Initiative show that there is hope—even in the midst of HIV and AIDS," Princess Zulu told a magazine reporter. "I am living proof."

Few of us have the prominence of Joseph in Pharaoh's kingdom or the platform of Princess Zulu in the twenty-first century. Even so, as Christian counselors, we also can be God's chosen instruments for bringing hope, even when everything seems hopeless. This is a book about the hope that comes from Christ, hope that often is conveyed through dedicated Christian counselors. Our work may not be easy, but what could be more fulfilling than serving God by bringing encouragement and hopefulness to people in need! What may have been intended for evil, God can turn into good, often through the work of Christian counselors. Probably through you.

# Epilogue:
# The Rest of the Stories

Every counseling situation is unique, depending on the counselee, the counselor, the setting where the counseling occurs, and the distinctive characteristics of the problem. Because of these differences, there can be no one correct way to counsel. The stories that you have read in this book might have been handled in a variety of ways.

In this epilogue you will find a brief description of what the counselors did and what actually happened to each of the people who are described in the preceding pages of this book. This is a summary of the rest of the story for each counselee at the time when this book was published. If they become available in the future, we will try to post additional follow-up reports on the web site that accompanies this book.

## 1. The Changes in Counseling: The Story of Caroline

For Caroline, the rest of her story is still being written. With her admission to graduate school, she moved to a new community and now attends a church where counseling is respected. Her former pastor still is critical of her career choice.

As this book goes to press, Caroline is continuing her training as a graduate student. She juggles a busy schedule, meeting the needs of her young family, her studies, and her developing career. She did, indeed, learn the skills of self-defense and completed the training period at the residential treatment facility that was described above.

She still is convinced that this is not the type of environment where God will lead her to work, but she is glad for the training she had. In addition, she has a new respect for those who work with people who are overwhelmed by their many problems and who know only one way to respond—with violence. Like every counselor in training, Caroline is growing. Her professors predict that she will become a competent counselor, in part because she is not afraid to take risks and to change.

## 2. The Counselor and Counseling: The Story of Sergio

As counseling continued, Sergio understood that depression is not a sign of weakness but often can be a symptom of something more. The medicine speeded up the recovery process while Sergio and the counselor met for ten weekly sessions. Part of this involved monitoring the medicine intake, encouraging Sergio to get exercise, and working on his self-esteem and identity issues. The healing continued as Sergio began to understand what was going on in his life and as he was helped to deal with the spiritual emptiness and emotional struggles in his life. Eventually the sessions got less frequent and the counseling was terminated. Recently the counselor met Sergio at a church meeting. He was still the youth pastor of the same church, but now with a group of eight hundred young people. There had been no further moral lapses or recurrence of the depression and guilt.

## 3. The Church and Counseling: The Story of Pastor Glen

Glen is still in the ministry and still finds fulfillment in his work and calling. When he was interviewed for this book, Pastor Glen said several times, "I don't have the answers yet," but he admitted that counseling was the part of his work that he likes the best. His church is trying to become more emergent but "that takes time," Glen said. "Trying to move a church in a new direction is like turning a large ocean liner. It takes a lot of time and effort." There is progress, but it is slow.

Regarding the three homeless people, the couple were given temporary help by the Temporary Assistance Program, then they disappeared from the community. Glen spent over two hours trying to make arrangements for the mother and her daughter to find housing. A local Christian center found them a temporary home and everything was arranged, but the mother and daughter failed to show up at the appointed time to get the help they had requested. Glen felt that he has wasted a lot of his time and energy trying to help. The man in the car tended to be afraid and distrusting. One morning when Glen and his staff arrived at the church, the car was gone and so was the man. Glen continues to minister to these kinds of "drop in" people, and some members of the congregation are beginning to see the value and need for this kind of caring ministry. A few weeks following this interview, Glen accepted an invitation to be volunteer chaplain for the local police department. He responds to emergency calls and often finds himself counseling people in times of crisis. He considers this to be a part of his ministry and an extension of the work of his church. It also is a model for the members of his congregation.

## 4. The Community and Counseling: The Story of Yvette

In the two years since the caseworker referred Yvette to Community Counseling Services she has made slow but significant progress. The CCS environment, the Mothers' Group, and Yvette's involvement with the church and its mentor program have given her support, hope, skills, and guidance when she has needed it. Recently in the group she learned about a job-training program that she now has joined. Currently she is learning computer skills and hopes to get a better job with her new knowledge. Most important, Yvette has learned that she is not an island, that she needs other people to survive, and that caring people are available. She now has an awareness of God's love and of the support that can come from a church that has a commitment to community needs and outreach. After her long period of hesitation to build relationships with others, Yvette has built a friendship with another woman in the Mothers' Group. Now Yvette has someone to talk to when she is upset, and someone to watch her kids when she needs a break. She is hopeful that with the support she is now receiving, she will never again get to the point of hurting her children and her children will not repeat the destructive coping patterns that Yvette initially learned from her mother.

### 5. The Core of Counseling: The Story of Bob

The counselor began working with Bob and his wife together. With her help, Bob was able to express his emotions more freely. The couple learned to talk about their feelings, and whenever he felt tempted sexually, Bob agreed to tell his wife. Their own sexuality as a couple improved, and the pull of the computer pornography subsided significantly. Bob still has temptations, especially when he feels lonely or discouraged, but he senses a closer relationship with God. It took a while, but in time he was able to forgive the man who mistreated him at the boarding school and the missionaries there who taught him to stifle his feelings. Sometimes the old pain returns, especially when he is reminded about his past, but he talks with his wife and his counselor friend and he sees that the events from his past are having less and less control over him as the years pass. "We run into each other from time to time," the counselor wrote along with his story for this book. Like most men, Bob has sexual temptations at times and sometimes he hides his emotions, but "he told me he now has control over his desires, and that God had blessed his ministry in ways he never expected." Bob and his wife are still missionaries and still friends with the missionary counselor who provided this story and with the counselor's family.

### 6. Legal, Ethical, and Moral Issues in Christian Counseling: The Story of Matt

This case is still in progress. At last report, Matt and his original counselor were still meeting. Matt's depression was lessening, and he felt accepted by the counselor. The counselor had not encouraged Matt to get involved in the gay community, but neither had the counselor revealed his perspective or referred Matt to a counselor who was more sympathetic to Matt's sexual orientation. The current counselor reports that "this decision is the hardest that I have encountered in my counseling practice" because the counselor believes that to refer Matt, to encourage Matt's homosexuality, and to have the counselor bring his own views into the counseling can all have an adverse influence on the client at this point. "I struggle with this every day," the counselor reported. "I have prayed about it a lot." It is very difficult to know what to do. If you were having lunch with this counselor, what would you encourage him to do? Remember, legal, ethical, and moral issues rarely have easy answers.

## 7. Multicultural Issues: The Stories of the Rodriguez Family and the Families of Hamadi, Amira, and Salima

In seeking to help Jorge and his parents, the counselor sought to learn what might be culturally appropriate in working with a Hispanic family. Mrs. Rodriguez confirmed that she and her husband came from a cultural background in which the husband often is viewed as being in charge. The counselor suspected that Mr. Rodriguez felt marginalized and disrespected by the counseling process that a community agency had initiated. His wife had made the first contact with the counselor. He had not been consulted but, instead, had felt dragged into the situation. With an awareness of this, the counselor visited the husband, met with him privately, listened to him and showed respect, affirmed his importance in the family and especially in the life of his son, and requested his involvement. Mr. Rodriguez responded positively to this approach and returned to counseling, where the counselor focused on teaching parenting and communication skills. The family's Hispanic roots were affirmed at every opportunity, and the husband was helped to see that, while he was the leader of the family, his wife was a partner in the parenting relationship. In talking with Jorge, the counselor discovered that the boy felt unaccepted at the school where the other kids sometimes joked about his Hispanic background. Jorge needed help in connecting with the culture, so the school partnered with the family in working on this process. With this more open communication and awareness, things began to improve both in the home and at the school.

Because of the male dominance in Hamadi's culture, the counselor (who is male) began meeting with him over coffee—strong Arabic coffee—for a man-to-man discussion. The counselor affirmed Hamadi's dilemmas and agreed to help him solve some of the problems within the American culture where he and his family now lived. A female counselor was enlisted to work with the women, and a woman physician agreed to give a thorough medical examination and any needed treatment to Salima. After Salima was able to tell her husband about the rape, he agreed to abstain from sex with his wife for a specified period of time. Central to the counseling was the enlistment of a volunteer family that agreed to care for Salima, encouraging her and helping her adjust to her new culture. As a result of these interventions, Hamadi and his family seem less overwhelmed and better adjusted. They are still Muslims, but they have a new appreciation and respect for the Christian care-givers who have helped in their time of crisis. At last report the family is adjusting adequately and thinking of moving to a part of the United States that is warmer than the northern city where they still live.

## 8. Depression: The Story of Jennie

Jennie's counselor discovered that her physician had prescribed anti-depressant medication, and this was continued under the doctor's direction. The counselor did not see any evidence of suicidal tendencies, so the treatment went forward in several ways. First, Jennie and the counselor looked at the cycles in her life—the tendencies to set high expectations for herself, to conclude that she never could be good enough, and the subsequent self-sabotaging of everything she set out to accomplish. To help her break that cycle, the counselor suggested that Jennie should "create a new story for the rest of her life." He asked her to write out the new story, urged her to imagine what she could become, and helped her set new and realistic expectations for the future. In the process, the therapeutic relationship emerged as an association where a strong male (her counselor) encouraged her and did not repeatedly disparage her efforts. As Jennie got better, she learned how to challenge her father's negative assessments and to recognize that she had given him too much power to control her life. The counselor did not intervene in any uniquely Christian ways, but Jennie knew about his beliefs and saw his commitment to Christ in ways that were different and more positive than what she had experienced. Eventually, Jennie looked for a job in the field where she really wanted to work. After a couple of years she opened her own business and, at last report, was doing well, free of the debilitating depression, and no longer telling herself that she as a person or that her activities in life are "not good enough."

## 9. Anxiety: The Story of Zoe

The counselor began by teaching Zoe relaxation skills, including ways to breathe more deeply and to sleep more easily. When the counselor suggested that medication might be of help, Zoe resisted for months but finally agreed and discovered that she was more relaxed. In addition, with medication she was better able to remember the new perspectives and skills that she was gaining through counseling. Over the months that they worked together, the counselor and counselee worked at changing Zoe's attitudes, expectations of herself or others, and thoughts that were creating anxiety. This enabled her to develop a more realistic study pattern, to feel more at ease with her grades, and to let go of the judgmental and otherwise negative viewpoints that were hurting her relationships. All of this contributed to lower levels of anxiety.

Concerning the spiritual struggles, Zoe's counselor pointed out places in her life where she sometimes acted on faith and had found that this worked very well. Together they discussed the logical issues concerning Christianity, and the counselee was urged to make a leap of faith. She never made this decision, but she did move in that direction over time. The counselor wrote, "I hope this was a stepping stone in her journey toward Christ."

## 10. Anger: The Story of Mr. J

Counseling was a new concept for Mr. J, but he came to the sessions without protest after he recognized that the counselor would treat him with respect and help him adjust to the new culture without demeaning his country of origin. In discussing this case, the counselor reported that he:

- Tried to raise awareness in Mr. J about the ways in which his anger and anger expressions were having an adverse impact in his life and the life of his family.
- Helped Mr. J understand the causes of his anger and why he responded in the ways he did.
- Avoided confrontational language but challenged some of Mr. J's irrational beliefs, such as his conclusions that the visitors were bad people.

- Taught Mr. J some anger-management skills, including effective communication skills, self-talk, and ways to avoid bitterness and revenge.

After solid rapport had been built between Mr. J and his counselor, Salma also was brought into counseling, but with a female counselor. Can you think of reasons why Salma had a different counselor?

At last report, Mr. J is in better control of his anger, contact has been re-established with some of the neighbors, and a local company has agreed to give Mr. J one more chance to be employed. The tensions at work still persist but with less intensity and fewer negative results than the conflicts with prior employers had produced.

## 11. Guilt and Forgiveness: The Story of Raphael

The two men continued to meet whenever they could get together. The counselor held Raphael accountable for his behavior, and eventually he was able to join an accountability group close to where he lives. With the counselor's help, Raphael began to see that some of his drives, attitudes, and actions were a part of his sinful nature and that they had become sexually addictive. As he began to reexamine what he was believing, rethink the place of God's forgiveness in his life, and slowly begin to forgive himself, his visits to gay bars and places for gay sex occurred less and less frequently. He finally was able to talk to his wife about all of this. She felt hurt, disappointed, and angry, but she also went to a counselor and eventually was able to forgive Raphael, especially as she became aware that the changes in his life were genuine. As this book goes to press, over a year has passed since Raphael participated in gay sex. He does not state emphatically that he will never return, and he does admit to ongoing temptation at times. But the urges are considerably reduced. In writing this report the counselor added, "We still see each other when we are in the same city. Raphael and his wife have just had their third baby."

## 12. Loneliness: The Story of the Man Abandoned in Childhood

The storyteller in this chapter is a man whose healing still is a work in progress. He was enthusiastic about telling his story in hopes that it will help others, but he still feels isolation much of the time. Unlike all the other people who contributed case stories to this book, he did not want to read a final report of his story before the manuscript was sent to the publisher. He said that reading this would be too painful. His church gives him acceptance and human contact, but he does not get much of this from his family, friends, work, or living accommodations. Recently he began dating a single lady who is about his age and attends a different church, but the woman's pastor told her to end the relationship because this man is divorced. This has been devastating, but he continues to see the pastoral counselor, and he continues to be active at his church, where he has the social skills to interact appropriately with the other church attendees. He adds that he would value the prayers of the people who read and use this book.

## 13. Childhood: The Story of Vanessa

Vanessa's counselor met with the parents and affirmed their concern for her well-being in the midst of their marital problems. The parents were urged to keep their shouting and other overt conflict as far away from Vanessa as possible and to do what they could to provide a consistent environment. In addition, the parents were encouraged to reassure their daughter that they would not abandon her, that the divorce was not her fault, and that she would continue to see both her mother and her father. The parents were given practical ways to help them put these parenting principles into place.

With Vanessa, the counselor started every session with drawings and used play each time. This kept the environment consistent and allowed the counselor to monitor the child's concerns, feelings, experiences at home, and needs for reassurance. By making up new stories—some of which were shared with the parents later—the counselor helped Vanessa imagine a better future and take some steps to be in control of her circumstances and feelings. As Vanessa got older and more comfortable in the counseling room, she talked more about what she was experiencing and was more able to answer the counselor's general questions. There were setbacks at times, such as a new round of stress when the father started dating, but by using child-friendly techniques in the presence of a caring counselor, Vanessa was able to adjust relatively well as the parents separated, the father left, and the mother and daughter lived together.

## 14. Adolescence: The Story of Mark

Here is the counselor's report of what he did:

> I looked at Mark's behavior from a systems perspective. His behavior was nothing more than an issue of communication to other people in general, and his family in particular. In short, Mark was trying to communicate that he needed and wanted attention and connection with others—especially his dad. Although I met with the family as a whole to discuss boundaries, I spent the majority of my time working with the family in dyads. I met with Mark and his mother, Mark and his sister, and Mark and his brother. But by far the most fulfilling dyad was Mark and his father. While they were strangers at best during our initial sessions, Mark and his dad were able to find some genuine points of connection as a result of the counseling. As Mark started to connect with his family in significant ways, and as the family started to draw better boundaries as a unit, Mark no longer needed to act out at school.

After this chapter was written, the counselor was asked to give his response to the personal reflection question from this book, "Did you sense (like the author of this book sensed) that the counselor may even have enjoyed Mark's prank and the commotion that ensued?" The counselor replied "You are right. I did really end up liking this kid. I felt like he was so misunderstood by the school. And it made me laugh to see how he could manipulate the school uniform to look very much like a homeless person. Anyway, I liked that he was willing to go against the grain. He was not afraid to make a stir then stand back and watch the chaos." The counselor added, "Do you see any of my issues coming out in what I just said?" What do you think?

## 15. Twenties and Thirties: The Stories of Melissa and Phil

A physician prescribed anti-depressant medication for Melissa, and a counselor treated her with behavioral and cognitive methods. Melissa was helped to understand her family-of-origin issues, including her anger and grief. The counselor helped her develop new interpersonal skills, such as ways to be more assertive in setting up boundaries with her family. As the counseling helped Melissa think through her grace-based beliefs, she experienced a validation and solidifying of her new position. She also came to see that God would be pleased for her to choose a vocation that she would find fulfilling. She has continued to work at developing an adult-to-adult relationship with her parents, knowing that on some theological and vocational issues there may have to be an agreement to disagree. Melissa no longer takes anti-depressant medication, and the depression is no longer a problem.

Phil continues with his struggles. His doctor prescribed medication to reduce Phil's anxiety, but when he started seeing a counselor who was recommended by the insurance company, he was told to stop taking the medication and that he only needed to discipline his mind. Recently Phil has been able to connect with a few people in his church who are older and able to bring more stability into his world. Despite his personality quirks he is connecting better with a strong church community where he finds acceptance and clear accountability.

## 16. Forties and Fifties: The Story of Don

Without discouraging the novel-writing activities and aspirations, a counselor helped Don take a fresh look at his life, including his goals, strengths, hopes, and values. Even without a lot of encouragement from the counselor, Don has begun an academic program at a local college where he can attend night classes on a part-time basis. He does not seem bothered by the low quality of this school and by the fact that the courses will not transfer to more credible, accredited academic institutions. Don still does not have long-term goals and some-times lacks motivation to pursue goals, but the counselor continues to challenge Don and be encouraging. Don and his wife have shifted to a smaller, more compatible church where they feel more comfortable with the traditional worship style and where he can use some of his writing and care-giving strengths.

## 17. The Later Years: The Story of Dr. Rachel Jones

Dr. Jones responded well to brief and structured psychotherapy. One of the keys to her successful treatment for depression involved the counselor challenging her view that since she could not be physically active, she could not have a purpose in life. This included a process of grieving her loss of physical functioning.

The counselor worked with Dr. Jones to identify ways in which she could utilize her intellect to increase her sense of usefulness and social connectedness. Through coordination with the onsite social worker, Dr. Jones became a mentor for a high school student who was considering a career in healthcare. A second key to Dr. Jones' successful treatment was the use of reminiscence therapy. Dr. Jones completed a journal which included pictures and personal anecdotes. This allowed her to gain a sense that her life had indeed been worth living so far, and some insights into how she could continue to strengthen her legacy in the lives of others. Finally, the counselor helped Dr. Jones identify social activities which were still available to her despite her physical limitations. Dr. Jones was able to regain her assertiveness to make requests that her care-givers should help her maneuver the wheel chair out of her apartment and into the social milieu.

In reading this summary, how do you respond to the fact that Dr. Jones' Christian counselor makes no reference to anything Christian in the treatment?

## 18. Conflict and Relationships: The Story of Disagreement at Camp Sunrise

When the meeting reconvened, the leader of the younger group asked if he could make a suggestion on behalf of his team. As his group had agreed, this young man spoke positively and sincerely about the contribution of the older camp leaders and how they had guided the camp and influenced the lives of those younger people who were present. He reassured everybody that there was no intention to undermine the camp's biblical base or to shift away from the long-established purposes of bringing younger people to a growing relationship with Jesus Christ. With what surely was God-given wisdom, this youthful speaker humbly described how younger people had changed and indicated how the new leaders wanted to reach them. He proposed that for two weeks they try the new approach and then come together for an evaluation. "We will get feedback from the campers," he said, "and of course we can always go back." Reluctantly for some, everybody agreed and the crisis was averted for at least two weeks. As a reader of this book, can you guess what happened after that? Come up with your own answer to this question before you read on.

Probably you guessed that the kids in the camp loved the new approach. It was continued for the rest of the summer, and there has never been any return to methods that may have worked a few decades ago but that do not work now. Even the camp founders agreed that the new approach was an improvement. "These people were threatened by the change," said the counselor who shared this story. "Probably some of them knew that they had lost touch with the generation of the campers, but they had invested so much in this work and they were afraid that they would be pushed aside. Some may have thought that their contributions would not be appreciated and that their wisdom would be dismissed even though it had been built over the years through the mistakes that they had made." After the camp closed at the end of the summer, there was a banquet for the camp workers. The older leaders were affirmed by those who were younger, given gifts of appreciation, and assured that their active involvement in the camp would still be welcome and needed even as a younger group of leaders took a more active leadership role. Not all conflicts end smoothly. This one did.

## 19. Sex Apart from Marriage: The Story of Fred

After years of counseling, Fred realized that many of his sexual difficulties seemed to originate from his unresolved family-of-origin issues. Thus his counseling has been focused on working through family issues as well as learning how to maintain sexual integrity. Fred, with counseling, was able to forgive Suzy, and they were both able to look back on their dating relationship, admit many things that they did wrong, seek forgiveness from God and each other, and learn from their experience. Fred and Suzy eventually ended their relationship and have moved on with their lives. With continued counseling, Fred is learning to face challenges in his life without the comfort that sex had falsely provided for so long.

## 20. Sex Within Marriage: The Story of John and Brenda

Here is the counselor's report of what happened with John and Brenda:

> I encouraged them to look at the Scriptures to see if there were any sexual boundaries that they could glean from the Bible. Of course the Bible offered few guidelines, so I asked them to refocus their sexual relationship on what was mutually fulfilling and gratifying. This was facilitated by several sessions with Brenda helping her deal with her own sexuality. I discovered that the sexual abuse (which she had mentioned almost in passing during the first session, implying that it was of little importance) actually was interfering with her sense of whether or not it was really alright for her to enjoy sex. As the couple counseling progressed, it became clear that John really was more concerned with having an exciting sex life than with any one particular type of sexual activity. Once Brenda started to free herself to enjoy sex, John was more satisfied with her investment. Their sexual relationship was not perfect by any means, but they did start to enjoy each other more passionately and the struggles over methods faded.

## 21. Homosexuality: The Stories of Julia and Billy

The counselor decided to work with Julia one on one without her parents being present. The counseling work began with a careful clarification of her goals and wishes, along with a clear indication about what counseling could or could not do. According to the counselor's notes,

> I made a genuine attempt to offer truly "informed consent" about the direction of our counseling conversations. I felt my role as her counselor was to inform her of what we know and don't know as it relates to her story. I told her that I could not explain why she feels the way she does nor why she is drawn to those of the same sex. I couldn't promise her that any counselor or any set of techniques or any medication would make these feelings go away. We discussed how God calls each of us to holy living and conformity to his will as revealed in his Word. After meeting for about ten sessions, we put together an answer to her initial question: "Am

I gay?" She concluded that she was not gay. As a young person, Julia is weaving together before God who she is and who she will become. When we met, she was in the midst of an intense period of development where she would be making choices, managing feelings, moving into new roles, and connecting in new relationships. Her destiny is to build her identity and future direction without letting feelings or attractions dictate that identity. After these brief explorations Julia had less fear about her impulses and more confidence about her ability to shape her future under God's loving care.

And what happened to Billy? His sexual attractions primarily were to men who appeared to have power, self-confidence, and strength. These were traits that Billy felt he lacked completely. With this knowledge, the counselor moved forward on three fronts. First, the counselor encouraged Billy to pray that he could recognize and acknowledge his own God-given strengths. Billy began to see himself in a different way with the skills, competencies, talents, and "great personality" that others saw in him but that he had not seen or been willing to acknowledge in himself. The more powerful and confident he felt, the less he felt an attraction to powerful men. Second, the counselor helped Billy see that there was a difference between having a sexual attraction to a man and having a close and intimate non-sexual connection with another male. Billy had confused emotional intimacy with sexual intimacy, assuming that any closeness to another male had to involve sexual feelings. Third, the counselor used the counseling relationship as a model of two men—including a counselor with the traits that Billy admired—who could work together to build a close bond that was not sexual. Since he never had a good relationship with his dad while growing up, Billy had almost no experience connecting in a close, nonsexual way with a powerful and self-confident man. The counselor provided that opportunity in a healthy way.

Did he ever totally stop getting an erection at the sight of a guy in a bathing suit? Not totally while he was in counseling, but he did begin to feel less overt attraction to men. Regrettably, the case had to be terminated because the counselor was moving to another location. Billy did not want to transfer to another counselor. He said that he liked the way in which his attraction to other men had been "framed," and he didn't want to go to another counselor and find out that this new frame wasn't true. He was afraid that another counselor might tell him he was gay, and he didn't want to take that chance. At last report, Billy was still in his ministry position.

## 22. Abuse and Neglect: The Story of Ms. K

As this book goes to press, Ms. K is still in counseling, where she has made many positive gains, particularly in the ability to control her self-harm instincts and to find healthier ways to cope. After several months of counseling, Ms. K was willing to tell a close friend about her past abuse and the ongoing pain that it has caused. Talking with a friend and accepting her support was a new and healing experience for Ms. K.

The most difficult part of the treatment has been helping Ms. K through her extreme and intrusive flashbacks or nightmares that hit her unexpectedly and severely. She can be haunted for days by a particular memory and fights to stay in the present when she is overwhelmed by the memory. The counselor has worked with Ms. K on ways to keep her grounded in present reality when this happens. They also have worked on Ms. K's feelings toward her parents, with whom she still has regular contact, moving toward discussion of how she might someday set better boundaries with them and confront their past and present denial of her pain. In addition, the counselor and Ms. K have been able to discuss her feelings toward her brother, and she has been able to express some of her emotions of anger, confusion, and hurt. Even so, she acknowledges that she is still a long way from the possibility of confronting him directly about the past.

Because of the counseling, Ms. K has increasingly been willing to consider her abuse as something that happened to a little girl who was in an emotionally unsafe home environment with a manipulative and powerful abuser. This is in contrast to her previous belief of herself as an "equal" partner in the abuse. She has also begun to consider the possibility that God hurts with her in her pain, slowly moving away from the unhealthy belief that God abandoned her because she deserved the abuse.

## 23. Inferiority and Self-Esteem: The Story of Mrs. A

Treatment for Mrs. A involved deepening her understanding of the internal, maladaptive processes that were impacting her life. Once she began to understand the causes of her inferiority and how it was maintained, Mrs. A was able (slowly) to change what she needed from other people. Helping her husband understand her ambivalence and her swings of dependency and fury enabled him to modify his behavior and to better understand his wife. Over time, Mrs. A's neediness lessened and her relationships matured, including her relationship with her husband.

## 24. Physical Illness: The Story of Paul

There is a surprising follow-up to this real-life story. When Paul was age twenty-three, a new drug was approved that attacked rheumatoid arthritis in a different manner. Paul was one of the first people to be allowed to take the new drug because he had tried everything else and nothing was working. Within a year, Paul's life was completely turned around. He felt that he had been given his body and his life back again. After being in virtually constant pain since he was six years old, Paul was surprised to find that it was difficult or odd to not be in pain—to no longer feel constant discomfort in his body. At the time of this writing, Paul is in his early thirties. Despite some minor ups and downs, his condition has continued to improve as a result of this new drug. He has resumed his involvement in sports, has completed college, is enrolled in a PhD program, and is actively involved in working with a not-for-profit organization that helps people who suffer because of severe physical illness or trauma.

## 25. Grief: The Story of Mrs. M

Counseling was short-term (about ten sessions), supportive, and educational in focus. The counselor worked specifically on helping Mrs. M adjust to her changed circumstances and helping her recognize that her grieving process was normal. Events such as forgetting she had taken the car related to having only one car for much of her married life. Her husband had driven the car almost exclusively, and she had frequently used public transportation. Assured that she actually was coping well with her responsibilities, Mrs. M felt encouraged and there was a rapid decrease in the anxiety about her functioning. With the counselor's help she felt increasingly able to negotiate with her sons and her church friends with regard to the timing and types of changes that needed to be made in her home and her life.

About two months after initially coming in, Mrs. M called one day to say that she would be late. She arrived somewhat disheveled and out of breath. Despite the counselor's initial concern, it soon became apparent that she was highly pleased with herself. It appeared that there had been a plumbing crisis in the morning. Initially this was overwhelming and left her momentarily furious with her husband for having left her alone. However, she worked through her anger, recognizing it as a normal grief reaction, and determined not to call her sons but to handle the situation herself. She was highly pleased that she had found a reputable plumber to do emergency repairs that morning and had arranged for ongoing work to take care of the problem long term. Not long after that, counseling was concluded.

## 26. Singleness: The Story of Susan

Counseling with Susan had a twofold focus. Initially she focused on finding contentment in her singleness and consciously taking responsibility for her own life. She worked specifically on what it meant to trust God in the details of life, including whether she would have a husband and children.

A second focus of counseling was longer term (about one year) as Susan worked on accepting herself as a valuable person without the affirmation of marriage or children. This was hard for her to do, but increasingly she was able to see herself as loved by God for who she was rather than for what she did for others. She came to recognize that her caretaking was often a way of putting herself down and seeking the affirmation of other people. With this realization, she was able to make better choices about what she wanted or felt that God really wanted her to do. This enabled her to set better limits at work and with her family. She was able to renegotiate her work style and was affirmed in that by her superiors. She continued to address her singleness in an ongoing process of finding daily contentment, while not limiting God for the future. She also chose to become involved as a mentor in a professional mentoring program where she currently mentors younger women in her career area.

## 27. Choosing a Marriage Partner: The Story of Jeff

Lisa had tried to be patient with Jeff, but she withdrew in response to Jeff's criticisms, hoping that a renewed relationship could form but knowing that her withdrawal could be the end. After about six weeks, Jeff's ongoing counseling, and a few very reformative conversations, Jeff and Lisa slowly began developing a new relationship. Many of Jeff's fears have dissolved, and he once again has been able to embrace and enjoy their relationship without critical monologue rolling through his head. She has felt supported, loved, and (as a result) comfortable in revealing more of herself. As this has happened, Jeff has seen more in her to love. There have been some struggles, with continued growth, but mostly they have felt joy and encouragement. As this book goes to press, Jeff is continuing with his counseling, dealing with some of the family and insecurity issues that he needed to address. The couple completed pre-engagement and premarital counseling to foster their relationship and to learn more about each other's perspective. They were married shortly before this book was published.

## 28. Premarital Counseling: The Story of Leslie and Tony

Leslie and Tony got married as they had planned, and they moved away from their home area. They now have been married for seven years. Both are employed, and Leslie is in graduate school. They have no children yet. Their marriage has been relatively good, but they continue to have money problems and difficulties in resolving conflicts.

## 29. Marriage Issues: The Story of Jack and Jill

The counselor agreed to work with this couple, but only if they would go through a ten-month anger-management/life-skills group program—one for perpetrators and the other for spouses. Using what the counselor called "a modified version of Short-Term Dynamic Psychotherapy," Jack was helped to gain the ability to understand, work through, and control his intense rage and its roots. This included a history of sexual and emotional abuse by a grandparent. Jack was not comfortable disclosing any of this until well into the middle phase of treatment. Through the counseling he was helped to deal with painful shame, guilt feelings, and his tendencies to jump into intense activity to avoid his fear of intimacy. With insight, touching, tender comfort, and understanding from his wife, Jack was able to grieve over his past and to allow himself to be more intimate in his marriage. At one point, Jill got several weeks of Cognitive Behavioral Therapy from a separate therapist in order to help her with boundary setting, appropriate self-care, and emotional stability.

This process has taken almost four years, and the road has not been easy. After three or four incidents of physical violence at the beginning, the abuse has stopped. On their own initiative, the couple stepped down from leading worship, and they now attend a different church. They have both grown spiritually. They pray comfortably, powerfully, and tenderly for and with each other. Sex is now an expression of love for each other, and they currently experience levels of emotional intimacy that few couples ever seem to reach. Jill now trusts Jack and appreciates his many strengths, but she encourages him in recreation and play as well. Jack appreciates Jill's newfound humility and trusts her love enough to take risks in getting close to her. At the time of this book's publication, Jill was pregnant, and she and Jack were looking forward to starting their family together.

### 30. Pregnancy Issues: The Story of Cindy and Tim

The counselor counseled with Cindy alone, had a session or two with Tim, and then worked with them together. Cindy discovered in counseling that she could let her guard down enough to acknowledge her pain. Although it wasn't easy, she talked through waves of grief, anger, jealousy, and disappointment that she had been carrying for many years. Cindy was able to reconnect with Tim on a more intimate basis as she realized that she was not a failure. In turn, she came to believe him when he told her that he did not blame her for their fertility problems; this was a fear that she had projected onto her husband for the past ten years. As Cindy and Tim expressed and experienced their grief together, they were able to focus on the gift of life that awaited them through adoption. In the meantime, they were able to talk about their discomforts being in the presence of friends who had children. As they relaxed in these situations, their friends relaxed as well, and tension in these social situations subsided. The adoption process was longer, more complicated, and more frustrating than they had anticipated, but eventually they brought home their three-month-old son. They named him Nathan, which means "Gift of God."

## 31. Family Issues: The Story of Pastor R and Tracy

Tracy was the catalyst that initiated change in Pastor R. After an especially frustrating day with incessant interruptions, she told her husband that the stream of visitors had to stop and that his family needed his attention at least as much as the people in his congregation. Somewhat shaken by Tracy's firmness, Pastor R had lunch with a friend from seminary, and together they talked over the family situation. As a start, Pastor R followed the example of his friend and started taking Thursdays away from his work. The family moved to a different house farther away from the church, and the stream of visitors eventually dried up. Recently the couple took a giant step for them and began seeing a counselor. Among the counselor's goals is showing Pastor R how to build better relationships at home, put limits on the demands that he piles on himself, and set boundaries so that he is not overwhelmed by the inconsiderate demands of the senior pastor.

## 32. Divorce and Remarriage: The Story of Peter and Mary

Based on what you have read thus far, do you think Peter and Mary got a divorce? Decide on your answer before you read further. At the time this book goes to press, the counselor will have been meeting with Peter on a weekly basis for about two years. Mary is in a Bible study, and although she has not made a commitment to Christ, she is open to spiritual growth and occasionally comes to church on Sunday and sits next to Peter. She had opposed divorce from the beginning.

Peter, in contrast, had maintained from the start of his counseling that the marriage was over. The pastor-counselor noted that God is at work in Peter's life, and Peter agreed. Even so, he continued to press the counselor for an answer to the divorce question. The counselor strongly urged Peter to keep working on the marriage but agreed, reluctantly, that the couple's sexuality had been damaged and that there did appear to be biblical grounds for divorce, even though he did not give his blessing or support to this alternative. Peter subsequently filed for divorce, and the couple is no longer married. They continue to get counseling and appear to maintain a friendship even though they divorced.

### 33. Mental Disorders: The Story of Mr. D

Mr. D's counselor has both theological training and a master's degree in counseling. Despite this background and experience, the counselor decided to refer Mr. D to a mental health professional who was more experienced and better able to deal with cases like this. It was clear that Mr. D functioned relatively well when he had appropriate medication, but he was more likely to hear voices, lose his temper, and resort to attention-getting techniques when he was not receiving the correct dosage. The new counselor partnered with a physician, and together they were able to help Mr. D function more adequately, despite what appeared to be evidences of schizophrenia, similar to what the counselee described in his mother. In all of this, the church was very supportive of this treatment and continued to welcome him into the community despite his divorce and sometimes unusual behavior. Mr. D has set more realistic goals for his business and appears to be functioning adequately in his work. Recently he came to visit the counselor who prepared this case. Mr. D appeared to getting along relatively well, even though he continues to see a counselor and needs to take medication to maintain his stability.

### 34. Alcohol–Related Problems: The Story of Marjorie

As treatment ensued, Marjorie began to experience inner healing and forgiveness as she saw her intrinsic value as one of God's children. With the encouragement of others in the group, and her strengthened relationship with God, she built enough courage to contact her sister and explain the lifestyle changes she was making and had made. Although the sister resisted at first, over time she was able to see that the changes in Marjorie were genuine, and eventually she was allowed to have contacts and visits with her daughter. Marjorie explained the reasons for her absence from the girl's life, said that she had never stopped loving her daughter, and asked for forgiveness and another chance to prove herself. Much to Marjorie's surprise, her daughter forgave her and is glad to have her mother back.

## 35. Addictions: The Story of VT

VT forgot the Budweiser and stayed with a program called No Longer Bound (*www.nolongerbound.com*). The web site describes this as "a faith-based drug and alcohol program for adult males ages 18 and up. No Longer Bound is a ten-month, long-term process of recovery. The purpose for our program is to provide an opportunity for the men in the program to learn to take responsibility for their own recovery and adopt a whole lifestyle change. No Longer Bound is a Non-Profit ministry based on the Biblical teachings of Jesus Christ." Participation in this program enabled VT to become sober and stay that way, get healing, understand who God is, and have meaningful accountability. Each participant in the program has a two-month probationary period and then, following evaluation, may be enrolled for seven additional months that involve counseling ("dealing with the past and being real about life"), inner healing, and learning to set boundaries. Like other participants in the program, VT learned to keep a journal, maintain a daily moral inventory, and be accountable for his spiritual growth, work ethic, and attitude. After completing the program, VT has remained drug free. He got married to a supportive and encouraging wife (who has agreed to this publication of his story), has enrolled as a full-time student in a Christian college where he is studying to be a counselor, and sometimes counsels fellow students who quietly come to him and discuss their problems with Internet pornography. At times, VT tells his story to groups of young people who can learn from a man who wasted many years of his life but who now is "no longer bound."

## 36. Financial Counseling: The Story of Brad and Sue

The counselor for this case was trained in financial counseling, not in clinical psychology. It became apparent early in the discussion that each individual really wanted to have someone outside the marriage side with them in the dispute on how to use the proceeds of the insurance settlement. The counselor did not feel at all comfortable or capable of dealing with this conflict. Instead, he listened attentively to both sides of this issue and tried to first impart some financial principles of savings, budgeting, and budget tracking. After the initial meeting, there were four subsequent meetings to work toward understanding the couple's combined financial position, their cash flow, and the development of a budget. It is here where the discussion broke down. Brad and Sue were not willing to do the legwork to track their expenses and develop a budget. While they saw the shortages from a cash-flow perspective, they were not willing to make changes to their discretionary spending patterns so that their overall financial situation would change. Both sides were immovable in the position that if only the other person would change they would be out of this trouble. Lacking clinical skills, the counselor did not feel competent to guide in the communication breakdown and stress buildups that were dividing them further and creating more conflict in their marriage.

The counseling sessions ended without any apparent changes in behavior or thinking in either Brad or Sue. In retrospect, the counselor concluded that it was the couple's attitude toward money that was the problem, not their financial means or the position they were in. They did, after all, have the resources to resolve these problems if they worked together. In the end, materialism, a reluctance to share what God had given to them, an unwillingness to lean on God for understanding, and a refusal to wait for God's provision combined to create increasing stress in their lives and on their marriage.

With this additional knowledge, how would you have intervened in more clinical ways to help Brad and Sue calm their tensions, communicate better, and get to a place where they could work together on finding a solution to their financial difficulties?

## 37. Vocational Counseling: The Story of TL

When he resigned from the Local Software Company, TL determined not to look back, to listen for gossip, or to talk about his former position. This determination to maintain his integrity and respect has helped him through a long period of unemployment. He does hear about the company, however, since he lives in the same community as the company and is reluctant to relocate until he finds a new position. After TL's departure, the new CEO who was hired dismissed a number of company leaders, including the two men who had started the rumors about TL. Apparently morale is still low and turnover is high, but the company still survives and TL is moving on. He has come to realize that there has been a lot of grief associated with his departure, but he is processing that with his counselor, and, in general, his attitude is positive. He genuinely believes that he and his family are better because of this difficult time in their lives. Unlike many of the cases in this book, which describe events and problems from the past, the case of TL is ongoing. Even as these words were being written, he was being interviewed as one of the finalists for a CEO position at another company. Eventually he turned down this possibility, and his search continues.

## 38. Crises: The Story of Margaret

To prevent any ethical conflicts or dual-relationship issues, Margaret and her employer agreed that she should get counseling in a clinic other than the counseling center where she worked. The counselor helped Margaret understand why she had responded like she did on the morning of her panic attack. There were significant similarities both in the appearance of the client, who looked like her former husband, and in his verbal abuse. From this Margaret was helped to identify some of the circumstances that might trigger similar anxiety at another time. Through cognitive behavioral methods, she was taught how she could avoid similar panic in the future. The counselor also reminded Margaret that this was a one-time incident, that she had been successful in functioning without unusual anxiety for several years, that she was now in a safe and supportive marriage, that she had a strong faith and supportive church friends, and that she now had additional inner resources to deal with future stress and abusive people like the man she met in the office. Independently, Margaret and her husband concluded that it might be better if she took a different job, and subsequently she moved to another position. When she read this chapter prior to publication, several years had passed since the incident in the office and the counseling that followed. Margaret wrote "there have been so many changes to my personal story over the years that it no longer seems mine. Still, it is a good story, a good reminder of what I went through and one that I pray will help others gain help and insight in their healing process."

### 39. Trauma, Terror, and Terrorism: The Story of Lourdes and Andre

Lourdes initially approached counseling with extreme reluctance and skepticism. It seemed as if counseling represented a relationship that asked for more vulnerability when she had none to give. The beginning phase of counseling focused on two aspects: safety and consistency. To allow her to experience counseling as a safe relationship, she was allowed to initiate the direction of counseling, her reluctance was acknowledged and accepted openly, the furniture arrangement and placement of chairs in the office remained unchanged, and every session started and ended on time. These things allowed her to experience counseling as predictable and safe. This helped to lower her overall distress when coming to the counseling sessions.

The second phase of counseling focused on helping her understand how the past had impacted the present and how she could identify situations that might trigger traumatic stress. She also was helped to become aware of the physiological reactions that might occur in response to distress in the future. The counselor did all of this by encouraging Lourdes to talk through her past in her own words and at her own speed. When this was completed, the counselor and counselee began to look at events in her week and to see how they followed a similar sequence: *cues* that resemble trauma (playground), *emotions* that are generated (fear and emptiness), and *behavior* (intense cleaning of the home and/or sexual fantasies of impersonal sex). In tracking this sequence, Lourdes became more aware of the pattern and was able to see opportunities to do something different. Along with this tracking, the counselee also was shown how to pay attention to her physiological responses such as the elevated heart rate, sweating palms, and restlessness she experienced in response to stressful situations. Lourdes was taught ways to lower her level of arousal through relaxation exercises and spiritual disciplines.

As counseling progressed, Lourdes reported decreased traumatic distress, decreased sexual fantasies and cleaning, increased intimacy with her spouse, increased ability to interact freely in the community, lowered blood pressure, and increased overall health (as reported by her physician). The third and final phase of treatment was preparation for termination. This was difficult for Lourdes because she doubted that she could support herself. Open discussions about termination, discussing the use of other resources (such as involvement in a small group), and talking through her fears were all instrumental in helping her to be able to end the counseling.

## 40. Other Issues: The Story of Mary Ellen

Mary Ellen's story is an ongoing case. We cannot give a report about what happened because at this point only God knows the end result. Mary Ellen now agrees that she has an eating disorder, and she is making progress toward healthier exercise and eating habits. As she lets go of the eating disorder, however, she is getting more in touch with her feelings. She realizes that she has spent her life pleasing everybody, but in spite of her job, which she does not like, she has no understanding of who she is, her strengths, or what she would like to do with her life. As her personality has become less passive, marriage problems have emerged. The husband has been "super supportive" as long as the problems have been all about Mary Ellen, but she is beginning to resent the fact that he, too, has feelings that do not seem to get expressed. "I don't know what our marriage is based on," she told the counselor. "What is our foundation?" She sees the need for marriage counseling, but her husband refuses to go because he knows that the focus will be on him as well as on Mary Ellen's feelings and struggles.

Where is God in all of this? Mary Ellen feels guilty about her past. She views her eating disorder as a sinful addiction that she has chosen and hung on to. She feels a lot of shame and has difficulty accepting the grace and forgiveness of God. She and her husband go to church, but she "sits in the guilt" that she feels there. In the support group that Mary Ellen attends, she finds comfort and a better ability to accept God's grace and acceptance, especially when her counselor prays at the end.

Is there hope for Mary Ellen and her husband? You can decide. At this point the counselor is encouraged about the progress thus far and optimistic about the outcome.

## 41. Spiritual Issues: The Story of Bonnie

Bonnie's pastor is described as a sensitive man who understands her struggles, meets with her periodically, and encourages her in her work with the counselor. During her struggles when the children were gone, the counselor helped Bonnie to see that the worries and ruminating about her weaknesses and failures could be a way for her ADD mind to focus and to avoid the chaos of a week with no structure or demands. Bonnie was encouraged to check again with her physician to be sure that she was taking the most effective dosage of attention deficit disorder (ADD) medications.

In describing his approach to this case, the counselor said that his focus was on helping Bonnie restructure her thinking. As a Christian, he understood that much of Bonnie's struggle was spiritual, the result of some unhealthy teaching in the past but currently the influence of demonic voices telling her that she was not forgiven, not loved, not valued by God. The counselor reminded Bonnie of the truths that she knew but that she had allowed to be replaced by lies. She was enabled to get a more realistic picture of what God is really like. She was helped to refocus her thinking on the facts that she is doing a good job as a parent (not perfect but good), that God loves her and is forgiving, that he has blessed her with a number of opportunities and skills, and that she is not faultless but that nobody is except God. In counseling, Bonnie was helped to forgive her former husband and herself. After several counseling sessions Bonnie told her counselor that she sensed "God is telling me to lighten up on myself, that I can have a relationship with Jesus who is fun-loving, and that he understands my quirkiness and will help me to live with that." Bonnie is trying to get more connected with people in her church and even to relax with other believers rather than being consumed all the time with her kids, her work, and her worries.

## 42. Counseling the Counselor: The Story of the Anonymous Counselor

Here is the counselor's follow-up account of what happened.

The events described in this chapter happened early in my counseling career. I had been raised in a church where we were urged to "burn out for Jesus," to "work for the night is coming" when souls will be lost forever if we are not aggressively serving all the time. I was in a Christian environment where that spiritually driven mentality impacted everyone. We were all workaholic counselors, and like everybody else, I felt the need to be giving all the time, meeting as many needs as I could. I had accepted the idea that the recovery of my counselees depended on me, and I felt guilty when I was not there to give help.

The change in my life did not come from formal counseling. It came when I started sharing with another counselor who had been a fellow classmate in graduate school. Slowly I began to realize that I needed balance in my life. I needed boundaries. I needed time off, more of a social life. My friend helped me to see that I had limits, that God was in control of my clients and not me. My job was not to save the world but to be an instrument in God's hands to work in the lives of the people he brought into my office. I had taken on too much emotionally and personally. I started spending more quiet time with God and soon concluded that I needed to be working in a healthier environment. Eventually I quit my job, found employment elsewhere, and today have a healthier perspective on my role as a Christian counselor.

## 43. Counseling Waves of the Future: The Stories of Kevin and Nadette

Kevin has continued to attend the same church. "I told him that he needed consistency in his life," the pastor reported, "and I did something that I rarely do: I insisted that he be in church every week. It seems to be working." Kevin likes the worship style, the teaching, and the pastor's efforts to connect with younger people who have no church background. Perhaps most of all, Kevin likes the focus on caring and building relationships. The congregation has a number of older, more mature Christians who give support, encouragement, periodic challenges, and theological stability to people like Kevin, but most of the worshipers are in their twenties. They hang out together, sometimes have Bible studies, pray together, and know that the church is always open and a place where they can drink coffee with their friends and be connected online. Kevin still needs to get direction for his life. He still needs to refine some of his attitudes and change some of his behaviors. He needs to be less impulsive, but there is progress in that area, in part because so many people in the community have urged him to be less impulsive and have encouraged him when he shows evidence of consistency. Further help has come from a counselor who understands how Kevin thinks and who stays with him, like a counselor-mentor walking alongside a young counselee-protégé as he bounces through the ups and downs of life. Kevin now shares an apartment with some other guys who go to his church. They are all growing. They all have a long way to go. But they are making progress, in part because of their journey together in Christian community.

In Africa, thousands of miles away from where Kevin lives, Nadette's counselor gave this sobering follow-up to her story:

*There was no follow-up with this young woman.* She was one of many who had suffered incredibly from the war. Her testimony was not at all unusual. But it would have been entirely inappropriate for me to single her out and counsel her. In this type of setting there is considerable competition for anything perceived as a resource, so it would not have been appropriate to talk with her privately. To complicate issues, foreigners are often forbidden to work with former child soldiers, so for the reader of this case, there is the frustration of not knowing what really happened with Nadette. It should be noted that I met her and talked with her as she participated in several focus group discussions where other girls and women were sharing similar stories and verbalizing struggles about their past and their present circumstances.

Concerning child soldiers, there is a need for forgiveness for both boys and girls. However, the issues are more complicated for girls because of the sexual violations. As a result of this they are less likely to get a "good marriage." Even though it is known that the girls were abducted, they are still often (but not always) stigmatized. Additionally, females have very low status in this country, and female children even less. As they get older it seems that the boys are more likely to have problems with drug addiction, although I have the impression that they are likely to start using drugs while they are in the armed group. A big consideration in the case of these former child soldiers is what forgiveness would look like. It is NOT merely a case of forgiving oneself—the collective culture and traditional practices mean that experiencing forgiveness involves others.

# Appendix:
# The Cases and Their Origins

Almost all the cases in this book are about real people who have had real problems and have been seen by real counselors. Great care has been taken to shield the identities of these people so that their privacy is protected and there is no exploitation of their personal experiences. To protect the people whose stories appear in this book and to hide the identities of their counselors, we have taken the following precautions.

## The Case Diversity

With only a few exceptions, all the people whose stories appear in this book are individuals or couples who actually exist. About fifteen of the cases are what might be called conglomerates. Here, details from the lives of two or three people have been combined into the story of one person. For example, we might have taken the family history of one person and combined this with problem details that appeared in another person. In this way the identity of both individuals is more likely to have been protected but without weakening or distorting the case story that has been presented.

About three-fourths of the stories are written by experienced counselors who have described one or more of their counselees. In some cases the counselees know that their stories are being included and have given their approval. The other cases are of people who do not know that they are in this book but who should be impossible to recognize because of our efforts, cited below, to hide identities. Most of the stories are told in the present tense—as if they are taking place now—even though the majority of these counselees really were seen by their counselors at an earlier time.

One quarter of the cases have come from direct interviews with counselees who have told their own stories. Some of these interviews are presented as first-person accounts, but in every case the story is included with each counselee's permission and subsequent approval of the case as it has been written. In almost every interview case, the counselee's spouse, counselor, and/or significant other person has agreed that the case can be included and has read and given approval of the relevant chapter before it appeared in print. In every one of these situations, the interviewed people and those who have written their own stories have spontaneously expressed pleasure in knowing that their experiences might help counselors, their counselees, and the people who will read this book.

## The Case Details

With three exceptions (see next paragraph), the stories in this book are written in such a way that the identities of the counselees are disguised. Most often this has been done by changing details in terms of counselee age, gender, place of birth, racial or ethnic characteristics, marital status, names, occupation, or other features that might otherwise reveal the person's true identity. Except for minor changes, the details of the problem are intact and describe events that actually occurred but perhaps in settings other than those that are described. Even the people who told their own stories made changes to hide their identities.

Among the three exceptions, at least one of these cases is the description of a person whose life story has been published. Two other cases are from people who frequently give public lectures about their previous problems and counseling experiences. One of these people has used a fictitious name in this book and the other, Princess Kasune Zulu, has agreed that her real name can be used because her story is so widely known. Each of these three people agrees that their identities will be detected by some readers of this book. They have allowed their stories to be told nevertheless.

## The Case Providers

To further protect identities, the people who provided the cases have agreed to remain anonymous. In this way no person who has been in counseling will know whether his or her counselor has submitted any cases. As we have indicated, most of the case providers are professional counselors. Three are pastors. In addition to being counselors, six of the case providers are professors in graduate counselor-training programs. Five of the cases have been provided by students in graduate counseling programs. Whereas most of these case providers are from the United States, about ten of the cases or case providers are from outside of North America.

To help insure the relevance and international flavor of the cases, the majority have been read, critiqued, and/or discussed by students, professors, and counselors, including some who do not live or counsel in the United States.

It is our hope that no readers will review a case in this book and conclude the case is about them. If you or any other person reads a case and concludes "that sounds like me," there is a very great likelihood that the case is not you. This is because what you are reading has been distorted deliberately in terms of details so that the real nature of these real cases is hidden. Stated succinctly, any resemblances to readers of this book are unintended and purely coincidental.